T0128548

PROMISES FROM GOD'S WORD

Book II

DR. JOHN THOMAS WYLIE

authorHOUSE®

AuthorHouse™
1663 Liberty Drive
Bloomington, IN 47403
www.authorhouse.com
Phone: 1 (800) 839-8640

Published by AuthorHouse 05/26/2020

ISBN: 978-1-7283-6296-0 (sc)
ISBN: 978-1-7283-6295-3 (e)

Contents

MISTAKES

MONEY

MOTIVES

OPPORTUNITIES

PARENTING

PATIENCE

PRAYER

PREJUDICE

PRESENCE OF GOD

PRIDE

PRIORITIES

PROCRASTINATION

PRODUCTIVITY

REBELLION

RECONCILIATION

REGRETS

REJECTION

REPENTANCE

REPUTATION

RESPECT

RESPONSIBILITY

REST

SALVATION

Introduction

SOME OF THE TIME it is elusive solutions (hard to find answers) to life's issues when we need them the most. "Promises From God's Word, (Book II)" is is a continuation from its previous "Book I,"and serves also as an assortment of promises from God's Word (The Bible) which are spiritual, inspirational, motivational, devotional which are designed as an important instrument for finding what God has to say about our specific needs or circumstances. Each topic throughout this publication is listed in alphabetical order from "M" through "S." Every section contains interesting inquiries regarding the matter, answers from Scripture (with references), and a promise from God's Word (Authorized King James Translation unless otherwise indicated).

It is the author's expectation that this reading and hope makes the Bible open, helpful, and accessible for all who reference its pages.

MARRIAGE

1. What are the keys to a happy, strong marriage?

"And if it seem evil unto you to serve the LORD, choose you this day whom ye will serve; whether the gods which your fathers served that were on the other side of the flood, or the gods of the Am'-or-ites, in whose land ye dwell: but as for me and my house, we will serve the LORD."

Husbands and wives should have a united purpose to serve the LORD.

(Joshua 24:15)

"Drink waters out of thine own cistern, and running waters out of thine own well."

"Share your love only with you wife."

(Proverbs 5:15)

"Marriage is honourable in all, and the bed undefiled: but whoremongers and adulterers God will judge."

Give honor to marriage, and remain faithful to one another in marriage. God will surely judge people who are immoral and those who commit adultery.

Faithfulness. Without faithfulness there is no real trust or intimacy.

(Hebrews 13:4)

"And he answered and said unto them, Have ye not read, that he whom made them at the beginning MADE THEM MALE AND FEMALE,"

"And said, FOR THIS CAUSE SHALL A MAN LEAVE FATHER AND MOTHER, AND SHALL CLEAVE TO HIS WIFE: AND THEY TWAIN SHALL BE ONE FLESH?"

"Wherefore they are no more twain, but one flesh. What therefore God hath joined together, let not man put asunder."

There is always commitment between husband and wife.

(Matthew 19:4-6)

"WE then that are strong ought to bear the infirmities of the weak, and not to please ourselves."

"Let every one of us please his neighbour for his good to edification."

We should please other. If we do what helps them, we will build them up in the Lord.

Sacrifice.

(Romans 15:1, 2)

"Submitting yourselves one to another in the fear of God."

"Wives, submit yourselves unto your own husbands, as unto the Lord."

"For the husband is the head of the wife, even as Christ is the head of the church: and he is the saviour of the body."

"Therefore as the church is subject unto Christ, so let the wives be to their own husbands in every thing."

"Husbands, love your wives, even as Christ also loved the church, and gave himself for it;"

"That he might present it to himself a glorious church, not having spot, or wrinkle, or any such thing; but that it should be holy and without blemish."

"So ought men to love their wives as their own bodies. He that loveth his wife loveth himself."

"For no man ever yet hated his own flesh; but nourisheth and cherisheth it, even as the Lord the church:"

"For we are members of his body, of his flesh, and of his bones."

"FOR THIS CAUSE SHALL A MAN LEAVE HIS FATHER AND MOTHER, AND SHALL BE JOINED UNTO HIS WIFE, AND THEY TWO SHALL BE ONE FLESH."

"This is a great mystery: but I speak concerning Christ and the church."

"Nevertheless let every one of you in particular so love his wife even as himself; and the wife see that she reverence her husband."

Husband and wife must submit to one another out of reverence for Christ.

This is what we mean by "Mutual Submission."

(Ephesians 5:21-33)

"THOUGH I speak with the tongues of men and of angels, and have not charity, I am become as sounding brass, or a tinkling cymbal."

"And though I have the gift of prophecy, and understand all mysteries, and all knowledge; and though I have all faith, so that I could remove mountains, and have not charity, I am nothing."

"And though I bestow all my goods to feed the poor, and though I give my body to be burned, and have not charity, it profiteth me nothing."

"Charity suffereth long, and is kind; charity envieth not; charity vaunteth not itself, is not puffed up,"

"Doth not behave itself unseemly, seeketh not her own, is not easily provoked, thinketh no evil;"

"Rejoiceth not in iniquity, but rejoiceth in the truth;"

"Beareth all things, believeth all things, hopeth all things, endureth all things."

"Charity never faileth: but whether there be prophecies, they shall fail; whether there be tongues, they shall cease; whether there be knowledge, it shall vanish away."

"For we know in part, and we prophesy in part."

"But when that which is perfect is come, then that which is in part shall be done away."

"When I was a child, I spake as a child, I understood as a child, I thought as a child: but when I became a man, I put away childish things."

"For now we see through a glass, darkly; but then face to face: now I know in part; but then shall I know even as also I am known."

"And now abideth faith, hope, charity, these three; but the greatest of these is charity."

"Love will last forever."

(I Corinthians 13:1-13)

"Confess your faults one to another, and pray one for another, that ye may be healed.

The effectual fervent prayer of a righteous man availeth much."

Confess your sins to one another and pray for each other.

Communication.

(James 5:16)

"Give her of the fruit of her hands; and let her own works praise her in the gates."

Reward her for all she has done. Let her deeds publicly declare her praise.

A desire to constantly build each other up, to enhance each other's value.

(Proverbs 31:31)

"Let the husband render unto his wife due benevolence: and likewise also the wife unto the husband."

The husband should not deprive his wife of sexual intimacy...nor should the wife deprive her husband.

(I Corinthians 7:3)

"Let him kiss me with the kisses of his mouth: for thy love is better than wine."

"Because of the savour of thy good ointments thy name is as ointment poured forth, therefore do the virgins love thee."

"Draw me, we will run after thee: the king hath brought me into his chambers: we will be glad and rejoice in thee, we will remember thy love more than wine: the upright love thee."

"While the king sitteth at his table, my spikenard sendeth forth the smell thereof."

"A bundle of myrrh is my well beloved unto me; he shall lie all night betwixt my \

breasts."

A Healthy Sex Life.

(Song of Songs 1:2-4; 12, 13)

2. What blessings can a good wife or a good husband bring to each other?

"Who can find a virtuous woman? for her price is far above rubies."

"The heart of her husband doth safely trust her, so that he shall have no need of spoil."

"She will do him good and not evil all the days of her life."

"She seeketh wool, and flax, and worketh willingly with her hands."

"She is like the merchants' ships; she bringeth her food from afar."

"She riseth also while it is yet night, and giveth meat to her household, and a portion to her maidens."

"She considereth a field, and buyeth it: with the fruit of her hands she planteth a vineyard."

"She girdeth her loins with strength, and strengtheneth her arms."

"She perceiveth that her merchandise is good: her candle goeth not out by night."

"She layeth her hands to the spindle, and her hands hold the distaff."

"She stretcheth out her hand to the poor; yea, she reacheth forth her hands to the needy."

"She is not afraid of the snow for her household: for all her household are clothed with scarlet."

"She maketh herself coverings of tapestry; her clothing is silk and purple."

"Her husband is known in the gates, when he sitteth among the elders of the land."

"She maketh fine linen, and selleth it; and delivereth girdles unto the merchant."

"Strength and honour are her clothing; and she shall rejoice in time to come."

"She openeth her mouth with wisdom; and in her tongue is the law of kindness."

"She looketh well to the ways of her household, and eateth not the bread of idleness.'

"Her children arise up, and call her blessed; her husband also, and he praiseth her."

"Many daughters have done virtuously, but thou excellest them all."

"Favour is deceitful, and beauty is vain: but a woman that feareth the LORD, she shall be praised."

"Give her of the fruit of her hands; and let her own works praise her in the gates."

(Proverbs 31:10-31)

"The heart of her husband doth safely trust in her, so that he shall have no need of spoil."

Her husband can trust her, and she will greatly enrich his life.

(Proverbs 31:11)

"She will do him good and not evil all the days of her life."

She will not hinder him but help him all her life.

(Proverbs 31:12)

"Live joyfully with the wife whom thou lovest all the days of the life of thy vanity, which he hath given thee under the sun, all the days of thy vanity: for that is thy portion in this life, and in thy labour which thou takest under the sun."

Whenever something aggravates or irritates you about your spouse, remember the blessings your spouse brings to you as well precious times, trust, fulfilled needs, satisfaction, helpfulness, and happiness.

(Ecclesiastes 9:9)

3. Why should we be careful whom we marry?

"Of the nations concerning which the LORD said unto the children of Israel, Ye shall not go in to them, neither shall they come in unto you: for surely they will turn away your heart after their gods: Solomon clave unto these in love."

The LORD had obviously instructed his people not to intermarry with those countries, on the grounds that the women they wedded would lead them to worship their gods. However, Solomon insisted on loving them at anyway.

(I Kings 11:2)

"For they have taken of their daughters for themselves, and for their sons: so that the holy seed have mingled themselves with the people of those lands: yea, the hand of the princes and rulers hath been chief in this trespass."

For the men of Israel have married women from these people and have taken them as wives for their sons.

So the holy race has become polluted by these mixed marriages.

(Ezra 9:2)

"Be ye not unequally yoked together with unbelievers: for what fellowship hath righteousness with unrighteousness? And what communion hath light with darkness?

The person we marry can build us up or destroy us. The Bible encourages us not to marry someone who is an unbeliever, because it is too easy for that person to tempt us away from our faith. And if we are marrying another believer, we still must be sure we are marrying for the right reasons.

(II Corinthians 6:14)

PROMISE FROM GOD

"FOR THIS CAUSE SHALL A MAN LEAVE HIS FATHER AND MOTHER, AND SHALL BE JOINED UNTO HIS WIFE, AND THEY TWO SHALL BE ONE FLESH."

As Scripture states: A man leaves his father and mother and is joined to his wife, and the two are united into one.

(Ephesians 5:31)

MERCY

4. To whom does God show mercy?

"Blessed are the merciful; for they shall obtain mercy."

God bless those who are merciful, for they will be shown mercy.

(Matthew 5:7)

"For as the heaven is high above the earth, so great is his mercy toward them that fear him."

Mercy is shown to those who fear and honor the Lord.

(Psalm 103:11)

"AND IT SHALL COME TO PASS, THAT WHOSOEVER SHALL CALL ON THE NAME OF THE LORD SHALL BE SAVED."

Mercy is given to only those who ask for mercy.

(Acts 2:21)

"When thou shalt hearken to the voice of the LORD thy God, to keep all his commandments which I command thee this day, to do that which is right in the eyes of the LORD thy God."

God shows mercy to those with sincere hearts.

(Deuteronomy 13:18)

"The LORD is merciful and gracious, slow to anger, and plenteous in mercy."

"He will not always chide; neither will he keep his anger for ever."

"He hath not dealt with us after our sins; nor rewarded us according to our iniquities."

He has not punished us for all our sins, nor does he deal with us as we deserve.

God has mercy toward those who do not deserve it.

(Psalm 103: 8-10)

"And he said, I will make all my goodness pass before thee, and I will proclaim the name of the LORD before thee; and will be gracious to whom I will be gracious, and will shew mercy on whom I will shew mercy."

God shows mercy to anyone whom he chooses.

(Exodus 33:19)

5. How does God show us mercy?

"Bless the LORD, O my soul, and forget not all his benefits:"

"Who forgiveth all thine iniquities; who healeth all thy diseases;"

"Who redeemeth thy life from destruction; who crowneth thee with lovingkindness and tender mercies;"

"Who satisfieth thy mouth with good things; so that youth is renewed like the eagle's."

"The LORD executeth righteousness and judgment for all that are oppressed."

"He made known his ways unto Moses, his acts unto the children of Israel."

Dr. John Thomas Wylie

"The LORD is merciful and gracious, slow to anger, and plenteous in mercy."

"He will not always chide: neither will he keep his anger for ever."

"He hath not dealt with us after our sins; nor rewarded us according to our iniquities."

"For as the heaven is high above the earth, so great is his mercy toward them that fear him."

"As far as the east is from the west, so far hath he removed our transgressions from us."

"Like as a father pitieth his children, so the LORD pitieth them that fear him."

"For he knoweth our frame; he remembereth that we are dust."

"As for man, his days are as grass; as a flower of the field, so he flourisheth."

"For the wind passeth over it, and it is gone; and the place thereof shall know it no more."

"But the mercy of the LORD is from everlasting to everlasting upon them that fear him, and his righteousness unto children's children;"

"To such as keep his covenant, and to those that remember his commandments to do them."

He has not punished us for all our sins, nor does he deal with us as we deserve.

God shows mercy to those who don't deserve it.

(Psalm 103:2-18)

"And the LORD passed by before him, and proclaimed, The LORD, The LORD God, merciful and gracious, longsuffering, and abundant in goodness and truth."

(Exodus 34:6)

"But God, who is rich in mercy, for his great love wherewith he loved us,"

"Even when we were dead in sins, hath quickened us together with Christ, (by grace ye are saved;)"

"And hath raised us up together, and made us sit together in heavenly places in Christ Jesus:"

"That in the ages to come he might shew the exceeding riches of his grace in his kindness toward us through Christ Jesus."

God is so rich in mercy, and he love us so much, that even while we were dead because of our sins, he gave us life.

(Ephesians 2:4-7)

"By mercy and truth iniquity is purged: and by the fear of the LORD men depart from evil."

Unfailing love and faithfulness cover sin.

(Proverbs 16:6)

"Not by works of righteousness which we have done, but according to his mercy he saved us, by the washing of regeneration, and renewing of the Holy Ghost;"

God saved us not because of the good things we did, but because of his mercy.

(Titus 3:5)

6. Does God expect us to be merciful?

"He hath shewed thee, O man, what is good; and what doth the LORD require of thee, but to do justly, and to love mercy, and to walk humbly with thy God?

God saved us not because of the good things we did, but because of his mercy.

(Micah 6:8)

"But if ye had known what this meaneth, I WILL HAVE MERCY, AND NOT SACRIFICE, ye would not have condemned the guiltless."

God wants us to be merciful; He does not want our sacrifices.

(Matthew 12:7)

"Shouldest not thou also have had compassion on thy fellowservant, even as I had pity on thee?

Shouldn't you have mercy on your fellow servant, just as I had mercy on you?

(Matthew 18:33)

"Keep yourselves in the love of God, looking for he mercy of our Lord Jesus Christ unto eternal life."

"And of some have compassion, making a difference:"

"And others save with fear, pulling them out of the fire, hating even the garment spotted by the flesh."

We must show mercy to those whose faith is wavering...

(Jude 1:21-23)

PROMISE FROM GOD

"And his mercy is on them that fear him
from generation to generation."

His mercy goes on from generation to generation, to all who fear him."

(Luke 1:50)

MISTAKES

7. What does the Bible have
to say about mistakes?

"NOW the serpent was more subtil than any beast of the field which the LORD God had made. And he said unto the woman, Yea, hath God said, Ye shall not eat of every tree of the garden?"

"And the woman said unto the serpent, We may eat of the fruit of the trees of the garden:"

"But of the fruit of the tree which is in the midst of the garden, God hath said, Ye shall not eat of it, neither shall ye touch it, lest ye die:"

"And the serpent said unto the woman, Ye shall not surely die:"

"For God doth know that in the day ye eat thereof, then your eyes shall be opened, and ye shall be as gods, knowing good and evil."

"And when the woman saw that the tree was good for food, and that it was pleasant to the eyes, and a tree to be desired to make one wise, she took of the fruit thereof, and did eat, and gave also unto her husband with her; and he did eat."

"And the eyes of them both were opened, and they knew that they were naked; and they sewed fig leaves together, and made themselves aprons."

"And they heard the voice of the LORD God walking in the garden in the cool of the day: and Adam and his wife hid themselves from the presence of the LORD God amongst the trees of the garden."

"And the LORD God called unto Adam, and said unto him, Where art thou?"

"And he said, I heard thy voice in the garden, and I was afraid, because I was naked; and I hid myself."

"And he said, Who told thee that thou wast naked? Hast thou eaten of the tree, whereof I commanded thee that thou shouldest not eat?"

"And the man said, The woman whom thou gavest to be with me, she gave me of the tree, and I did eat."

"And the LORD God said unto the woman, What is this that thou hast done? And the woman said, The serpent beguiled me, and I did eat."

Both Adam and Eve responded to their mistakes by shifting the blame (fault).

(Genesis 3:1-13)

"AND the children of Israel did evil again in the sight of the LORD; and the LORD delivered them into the hand of the Phi-lis'-tines forty years."

"And there was a ceratin man of Zo'-rah, of the family of the Danites, whose name was Ma.no'-ah; and his wife was barren, and bare not."

"And the angel of the LORD appeared unto the woman, and said unto her, Behold now, thou art barren, and bearest not: but thou shalt conceive, and bear a son."

"Now therefore beware, I pray thee, and drink not wine nor strong drink, and eat not any unclean thing:"

"For, lo, thou shat conceive, and bear a son; and no razor shall come on his head: for the child shall be a Nazarite unto God from the womb: and he shall begin to deliver Israel out of the hand of the Phi-lis'-tines."

"Then the woman came and told her husband, saying, A man of God came unto me, and his countenance was like the countenance of an angel of God, very terrible: but I asked him not whence he was, neither told he me his name:"

"But he said unto me, Behold, thou shalt conceive, and bear a son; and now drink no wine nor strong drink, neither eat any unclean thing: for the child shall be a Nazarite to God from the womb to the day of his death."

Then Ma-no'-ah intreated the LORD, and said, O my Lord, let the man of God which thou didst send come again unto us, and teach us what we shall do unto the child that shall be born."

"And God hearkened to the voice of Ma-no'-ah; and the angel of God came again unto the woman as she sat in the field; but Ma-no'-ah her husband was not with her."

"And the woman made hast, and ran, and shewed her husband, and said unto him, Behold, the man hath appeared unto me, that came unto me the other day."

"And Ma-no'-ah arose, and went after his wife, and came to the man, and said unto him, Art thou the man that spakest unto the woman? And he said, I am."

"And Ma-no'-ah said, Now let thy words come to pass. How shall we order the child, and how shall we do unto him?"

"And the angel of the LORD said unto Ma-no'-ah, Of all that I said unto the woman let her beware."

"She may not eat of any thing that cometh of the vine, neither let her drink wine or strong drink, nor eat any unclean thing: all that I commanded her let her observe."

"And Ma-no'-ah, said unto the angel of the LORD, I pray thee, let us detain thee, until we shall have made ready a kid for thee."

"And the angel of the LORD said unto Ma-no'-ah, Though thou detain me, I will not eat thy bread: and if thou wilt offer a burnt offering, thou must offer it unto the LORD. For Ma'no'-ah knew not that he was an angel of the LORD."

"And Ma-no'-ah said unto the angel of the LORD, What is thy name, that when thy sayings come to pass we may do thee honour?"

"And the angel of the LORD said unto him, Why askest thou thus after my name, seeing it is secret?"

So Ma-no'-ah took a kid with a meat offering, and offered it upon a rock unto the LORD: and the angel did wonderously; and Ma-no'-ah and his wife looked on."

"For it came to pass, when the flame went up toward heaven from off the altar, that the angel of the LORD ascended in the flame of the altar. And Ma-no'-ah and his wife looked on it, and fell on their faces to the ground."

"But the angel of the LORD did no more appear to Ma-no'-ah and to his wife. Then Ma-no'-ah knew that he was an angel of the LORD."

"And Ma-no'-ah said unto his wife, We shall surely die, because we have seen God."

"But his wife said unto him, if the LORD were pleased to kill us, he would not have received a burnt offering and a meat offering at our hands, neither would he have shewed us all these things, nor would as at this time have told us such things as these."

"And the woman bare a son, and called his name Samson: and the child grew, and the LORD blessed him."

"And the Spirit of the LORD began to move him at times in the camp of Dan between Zo'-rah and Esh'-ta-ol."

"AND Samson went down to Tim'-nath, and saw a woman in Tim-nath of the daughters of the Phi-lis'-tines."

"And he came up, and told his father and his mother, and said, I have seen a woman in Tim'-nath of the daughters of the Phi-lis'-tines: now therefore get her for me to wife."

"Then his father and his mother said unto him, Is there never a woman among the daughters of thy brethren, or among all my people, that thou goest to take a wife of the uncircumcised Phi-lis'-tines? And Samson said unto his father, Get her for me; for she pleaseth me well."

"But his father and his mother knew not that it was of the LORD, that he sought an occasion against the Phi-lis'-tines: for at that time the Phi-lis'-tines had dominion over Israel."

"Then went Samson down, and his father and his mother, to Tim'- nath, and came to the vineyards of Tim'-nath: and, behold, a young lion roared against him."

"And the Spirit of the LORD came mightily upon him, and he rent him as he would have rent a kid, and he had nothing in his hand: but he told not his father or his mother what he had done."

"And he went down, and talked with the woman; and she pleased Samson well."

"And after a time he returned to take her, and he turned aside to see the carcase of the lion: and, behold, there was a swarm of bees and honey in the carcase of the lion."

"And he took thereof in his hands, and went on eating, and came to his father and mother, and gave them, and they did eat; but he told not them that he had taken the honey out of the carcase of the lion."

"So his father went down unto the woman: and Samson made there a feast; for so used the young men to do."

"And it came to pass, when they saw him, that they brought thirty companions to be with him."

"And Samson said unto them, I will now put forth a riddle unto you: if ye can certainly declare it me within the seven days of the feast, and find it out, then I will give you thirty sheets and thirty change of garments:"

"But if ye cannot declare it me, then shall ye give me thirty sheets and thirty change of garments. And they said unto him, Put forth thy riddle, that we may hear it."

"And he said unto them, Out of the eater came forth meat, and out of the strong came forth sweetness. And they could not in three days expound the riddle."

"And it came to pass on the seventh day, that they said unto Samson's wife, Entice thy husband, that he may declare unto us the riddle, lest we burn thee and thy father's house with fire: have ye called us to take that we have? is it not so?"

"And Samson's wife wept before him, and said, Thou dost but hate me, and lovest me not: thou hast put forth a riddle unto the children of my people, and hast not told it me. And he said unto her, Behold, I have not told it my father nor my mother, and shall I tell it thee?"

"And she wept before him the seven days, while the feast lasted: and it came to pass on the seventh day, that he told her, because she lay sore upon him: and she told the riddle to the children of her people."

"And the men of the city said unto him on the seventh day before the sun went down, What is sweeter than honey? And what is stronger than a lion? And he said unto them, If ye had not plowed with my heifer, ye had not found out my riddle."

"And the Spirit of the LORD came upon him, and he went down to Ash'-ke-lon, and slew thirty men of them, and took their spoil, and gave change of garments unto them which expounded the riddle. and he went up to his father's house."

"But Samson's wife was given to his companion, whom he had used as his friend."

"But it came to pass within a while after, in the time of wheat harvest, that Samson visited his wife with a kid; and he said, I will go in to my wife into the chamber. But her father would not suffer him to go in."

"And her father said, I verily thought that thou hadst utterly hated her; therefore I gave her to thy companion: is not her younger sister fairer than she? take her, I pray thee, instead of her."

"And Samson said concerning them, Now shall I be more blameless than the Phi-lis'-tines, though I do them a displeasure."

"And Samson went and caught three hundred foxes, and took firebrands, and turned tail to tail, and put a firebrand in the midst between two tails."

"And when he had set the brands on fire, he let them go into the standing corn of the Phi-lis'-tines, and burnt up both the shocks, and also the standing corn, with the vineyards and olives."

"Then the Phi-lis'-tines said, Who hath done this? And they answered, Samson, the son in law of the

Tim'-nite, because he had taken his wife, and given her to his companion.

And the Phi-lis'-tines came up, and burnt her and her father with fire."

"And Samson said unto them, Though ye have done this, yet will I be avenged of you, and after that I will cease."

"And he smote them hip and thigh with a great slaughter: and he went down and dwelt in the top of the rock E'-tam."

"Then the Phi-lis'-tines went up, and pitched in Judah, and spread themselves in Le'-hi."

"And the men of Judah said, Why are ye come up against us? And they answered, To bind Samson are we come up, to do to him as he hath done to us."

"Then three thousand men of Judah went to the top of the rock E'-tam, and said to Samson, knowest thou not that the Phi-lis'-tines are rulers over us? What is this that thou hast done unto us? And he said unto them, As they did unto me, so have I done unto them."

"And they said unto him, We are come down to bind thee, that we may deliver thee into the hand of the Phi-lis'-tines. And Samson said unto them, Swear unto me, that ye will not fall upon me yourselves."

"And they spake unto him, saying, No; but we will bind thee fast, and deliver thee into their hand: but surely we will not kill thee. And they bound him with two new cords, and brought him up from the rock."

"And when he came unto Le'-hi, the Phi-lis'-tines shouted against him: and the Spirit of the LORD came mightily upon him, and the cords that were upon his arms became as flax that were burnt with fire, and his bands loosed from off his hands."

"And he found a new jawbone of an ass, and put forth his hand, and took it, and slew a thousand men therewith."

"And Samson said, With the jawbone of an ass, heaps upon heaps, with the jaw of an ass have I slain a thousand men."

"And it came to pass, when he had made an end of speaking, that he cast away the jawbone out of his hand, and called that place Ra'-math-le'-hi."

"And he was sore athrist, and called on the LORD, and said, Thou hast given this grat deliverance into the hand of thy servant: and now shall I die for thirst, and fall into the hand of the uncircumcised?"

"But God clave an hollow place that was in the jaw, and there came water thereout; and when he had drunk, his spirit came again, and he revived: wherefore he called the name thereof En-hak'-ko-re, which is in Le'-hi unto this day."

"And he judged Israel in the days of the Phi-lis'-tines twenty years."

"THEN went Samson to Ga'-za, and saw there an harlot, and went in unto her."

"And it was told the Ga'-zites, saying, Samson is come hither. And they compassed him in the gate of the city, and were quiet all the night, saying, In the morning, when it is day, we shall kill him."

"And Samson lay till midnight, and arose at midnight, and took the doors of the gate of the city, and the two posts, and went away with them, bar and all, and put them upon his shoulders, and carried them up to the top of an hill that is before He'-bron."

"And it came to pass afterward, that he loved a woman in the valley of So'-rek, whose name was De-li'-lah."

"And the lords of the Phi-lis'-tines came up unto her, and said unto her, Entice him, and see wherein his great strength lieth, and by what means we may prevail against him, that we may bind him to afflict him: that we will give thee every one of us eleven hundred pieces of silver."

"And De-li'-lah said to Samson, Tell me, I pray thee, wherein thy great strength lieth, and wherewith thou mightest be bound to afflict thee."

"And Samson said unto her, If they bind me with seven green withs that were never dried, then shall I be weak, and be as another man."

"Then the lords of the Phi-lis'-tines brought up to her seven green withs which had not been dried, and she bound him with them."

"Now there were men lying in wait, abiding with her in the chamber. And she said unto him, The Phi-lis'-tines be upon thee, Samson. And he brake the withs, as a thread of tow is broken when it toucheth the fire. So his strength was not known."

"And De-li'-lah said unto Samson, Behold, thou hast mocked me, and told lies: now tell me, I pray thee, wherewith thou mightest be bound."

"And he said unto her, If they bind me fast with new ropes that never were occupied, then shall I be weak, and be as another man."

"De-li'-lah therefore took new ropes, and bound him therewith, and said unto him, The Phi-lis'-tines be upon thee, Samson. And there were liers in wait abiding in the chamber. And he brake them from off his arms like a thread."

"And De-li'-lah said unto Samson, Hitherto thou hast mocked me, and told me lies: tell me wherewith thou mightest be bound. And he said unto her, If thou weavest the seven locks of my head with the web."

"And she fastened it with the pin, and said unto him, the Phi'lis'-tines be upon thee, Samson. And he awaked out of his sleep, and went away with the pin of the beam, and with the web."

"And she said unto him, How canst thou say, I love thee, when thine heart is not with me? Thou hast mocked me these three times, and hast not told me wherein thy great strength lieth."

"And it came to pass, when she pressed him daily with her words, and urged him, so that his soul was vexed unto death;"

"That he told her all his heart, and said unto her, There hath not come a razor upon mine head; for I have been a Nazarite unto God from my mother's womb: if I be shaven, then my strength will go from me, and I shall become weak, and be like any other man."

"And when De-li'-lah saw that he had told her all his heart, she sent and called for the lords of the Phi-lis'-tines, saying, Come up this once, for he hath shewed me all his heart. Then the lords of the Phi-lis'-tines came up unto her, and brought money in their hand."

"And she made him sleep upon her knees; and she called for a man, and she caused him to shave off the seven locks of his head; and she began to afflict him, and his strength went from him."

"And she said, The Phi-lis'-tines be upon thee, Samson. And he awoke out of his sleep, and said, I will go out as at other times before, and shake myself. And he wist not that the LORD was departed from him."

"But the Phi-lis'-tines took him, and put out his eyes, and brought him down to Ga'-za, and bound him with fetters of brass; and he did grind in the prison house."

"Howbeit the hair of his head began to grow again after he was shaven."

"Then the lords of the Phi-lis'-tines gathered them together for to offer a great sacrifice unto Da'-gon their god, and to rejoice: for they said, Our god hath delivered Samson our enemy into our hand."

"And when the people saw him, they praised their god: for they said, Our god hath delivered into our hands our enemy, and the destroyer of our country, which slew many of us."

"And it came to pass, when their hearts were merry, that they said, Call for Samson, that he may make us sport. And they called for Samson out of the prison house; and he made them sport: and they set him between the pillars."

"And Samson said unto the lad that held him by the hand, Suffer me that I may feel the pillars whereupon the house standeth, that I may lean upon them."

"Now the house was full of men and women; and all the lords of the Phi-lis'-tines were there; and therewere upon the roof about three thousand men and women, that beheld while Samson made sport."

"And Samson called unto the LORD, and said, O Lord GOD, remember me, I pray thee, and strengthen me, I pray thee, only this once, O God, that I may be at once avenged of the Phi-lis'-tines for my two eyes."

"And Samson took hold of the two middle pillars upon which the house stood, and on which it was borne up, of the one with his right hand, and of the other with his left."

"And Samson said, Let me die with the Phi-lis'-tines. And he bowed himself with all his might; and the house fell upon the lords, and upon all the people that were therein.

So the dead which he slew at his death were more than they which he slew in his life."

"Then his brethren and all the house of his father came down, and took him, and brought him up, and buried him between Zo'-rah and Esh'-ta-ol in the buryplace of Ma-no'-ah his father. And he judged Israel twenty years."

Samson's life, although filled with foolish mistakes, was still mightily used by God.

(Judges 13:1-16:31)

"For in many things we offend all. If any man offend not in word, the same is a perfect man, and able also to bridle the whole body."

The most common mistake is saying something we later may regret.

(James 3:2)

"NOW the word of the LORD came unto Jonah the son of A-mit'-tai, saying,"

"Arise, go to Nin'-e-veh, that great city, and cry against it; for their wickedness is come up before me."

"But Jonah rose up to flee unto Tar'-shish from the presence of the LORD, and went down to Jop'-pa; and he found a ship going to Tar'-shish: so he paid the fare thereof, and went down into it, to go with them unto Tar'-shish from the presence of the Lord."

In this world, the worst mistake we can make is running from God.

(Jonah 1:1-3)

"And it came to pass in those days, when Moses was grown, that he went out unto his brethren, and looked on their burdens: and he spied an Egyptian smiting an Hebrew, one of his brethren."

"And he looked this way and that way, and when he saw that there was no man, he slew the Egyptian, and hid him in the sand."

"And when he went out the second day, behold, two men of the Hebrews strove together: and he said to him that did the wrong, Wherefore smitest thou thy fellow?"

"And he said, Who made thee a prince and a judge over us? intendest thou to kill me, as thou killest the Egyptian? And Moses feared, and said, Surely this thing is known.

"Now when Pharaoh heard this thing, he sought to slay Moses, But Moses fled from the face of Pharaoh, and dwelt in the land of Mid'-i-an: and he sat down by a well."

Even the life of Moses was marred by an immature and terrible mistake.

(Exodus 2:11-15)

"Now Peter sat without in the palace: and a damsel came unto him, saying, Thou also wast with Jesus of Galilee."

"But he denied before them all, saying, I know not what thou sayest."

"And when he was gone out into the porch, another maid saw him, and said unto them that were there, This fellow was also with Jesus of Nazareth."

"And again he denied with an oath, I do not know the man."

"And after a while came unto him they that stood by, and said to Peter, Surely thou also art one of them; for thy speech bewrayeth thee."

"Then began he to curse and to swear, saying, I know not the man. And immediately the cock crew."

"And Peter rememkbered the word of Jesus, which said unto him, Before the cock crow, thou shalt deny me thrice. And he went out, and wept bitterly."

Jesus Christ restored Peter to fellowship even after his most painful mistake.

(Matthew 26:69-75)

PROMISE FROM GOD

"Not as though I had already attained, either were already perfect: but I follow after, if that I may apprehend that for which also I apprehended of Christ Jesus."

"Brethren, I count not myself to have apprehended: but this one thing I do, forgetting those things which are behind, and reaching forth unto those things which are before."

"I press toward the mark for the prize of the high calling of God in Christ Jesus."

(Philippians 3:12-14)

MONEY

8. What is a proper perspective toward money?

"THE LORD is my shepherd; I shall not want."

The Lord is my shepherd; I have everything I need.

(Psalm 23:1)

"No man can serve two masters: for either he will hate the one, and love the other; or else he will hold to the one, and despise the other. Ye can not serve God and mammon."

You can not serve God and money.

The love of money can get our priorities out of line. We must keep reminding ourselves that God must be first in our lives and that money cannot satisfy our deepest needs.

(Matthew 6:24)

"But godliness with contentment is great gain.;"

"For we brought nothing into this world, and it is certain we can carry nothing out."

"And having food and raiment let us be therewith content."

But they that will be rich fall into temptation and a snare, and into many foolish and hurtful lusts, which drown men in destruction and perdition."

"For the love of money is the root of all evil: which while some coveted after, they have erred from the faith, and pierced themselves through with many sorrows."

For the love of money is the root of all kinds of evil.

(I Timothy 6:6-10)

"Let your conversation be without covetousness; and be content with such things as ye have: for he hath said, I WILL NEVER LEAVE THEE, NOR FORSAKE THEE."

(Hebrews 13:5)

"Incline my heart unto thy testimonies, and not to covetousness."

Money is not the root of all evil; the love of money is!

(Psalm 119:36)

"He that trusteth in his riches shall fall; but the righteous shall flourish as a branch."

Trusting in your money and soon you will find out one thing: DOWN YOU GO!!!

(Proverbs 11:28)

"Wherefore do ye spend money for that which is not bread? and your labour for that which satisfieth not? hearken diligently unto me, and eat ye that which is good, and let your soul delight itself in fatness."

Time after time we purchase things to fill a void or a need in our lives. The Bible focuses to an approach to procure a deep and lasting happiness that always satisfies.

(Isaiah 55:2)

"Better is the poor that walketh in his integrity, than he that is perverse in his lips, and is a fool."

It is better to be poor and honest than to be a fool and dishonest.

(Proverbs 19:1)

"For what shall it profit a man, if he shall gain the whole world, and lose his own soul?"

No measure of money is justified, despite all the trouble in the event that it was picked up deceptively, misleadingly or untrustworthily. Exploiting others to bring in money is stealing. The individuals who do this lose far more than they could ever gain.

(Mark 8:36)

"Not that I speak in respect of want: for I have learned, in whatsoever state I am, therewith to be content."

"I know both how to be abased, and I know how to abound; every where and in all things I am instructed both to be full and to be hungry, both to abound and to suffer need."

"I can do all things through Christ which strengtheneth me."

I have learned the secret of living in every situation.

(Philippians 4:11-13)

"But my God shall supply all your need according to his riches in glory by Christ Jesus."

The Bible promises that God will supply the entirety (all) of our needs. The issue comes when our meaning of "need" is not quite the same as God's. The principal thing we should do is study God's Word to find what he says we need for a fulfilling life.

(Philippians 4:19)

"And Jesus sat over against the treasury, and beheld how the people cast money into the treasury: and many that were rich cast in much."

"And there came a certain poor widow, and she threw in two mites, which make a farthing (about 50 cents)."

"And he called unto him his disciples, and saith unto them, Verily I say unto you, That this poor widow hath cast more in, than all they which have cast into the treasury:"

"For all they did cast in of their abundance; but she of her want did cast in all that she had, even all her living."

(Mark 12:41-44)

"But whoso hath this world's good, and seeth his brother have need, and shutteth up his bowels of compassion from him, how dwelleth the love of God in him?

Consistently and generously parting with our money may be the best method to shield us from loving it. When we see what giving does in the lives of others, needs are met in us that material belongings would never fulfill. This kind of giving measures our Christian love.

(I John 3:17)

"Honour the LORD with thy substance, and with the firstfruits of all thine increase:"

"So shall thy barns be filled with plenty, and thy presses shall burst out with new wine."

Honor the LORD with your wealth and with the best part of everything your land produces. Then he will fill your barns with grain...

(Proverbs 3:9, 10)

"Bring ye all the tithes into the storehouse, that there may be meat in mine house, and prove me now herewith, saith the LORD of hosts, if I will not open you the windows of heaven, and pour you out a blessing, that there shall not be room enough to receive it."

(Malachi 3:10)

"But this I say, He which soweth sparingly shall reap also sparingly; and he which soweth bountifully shall reap also bountifully."

The one who plants generously will get a generous crop.

(II Corinthians 9:6)

"There is treasure to be desired and oil in the dwelling of the wise; but a foolish man spendeth it up."

The foolish spends whatever they get.

(Proverbs 21:20)

"He that tilleth his land shall have plenty of bread: but he that followeth after vain persons shall have poverty enough."

Hard workers have plenty of food.

(Proverbs 28:19)

"For the kingdom of heaven is as a man travelling into a far country, who called his own servants, and delivered unto them his goods."

He called together his servants and gave them money to invest for him while he was gone.

(Matthew 25:14)

"And labour, working with our own hands: being reviled, we bless; being persecuted, we suffer it:"

We have worked wearily with our own hands to earn our living.

(I Corinthians 4:12)

"That ye may walk honestly toward them that are without, and that ye may have lack of nothing."

God urges us to be acceptable stewards in procuring, spending, and setting aside our money. He understands the significance of accommodating the necessities of our family and what's to come. Be that as it may, he likewise anticipates that we should use our money generously to help other people.

(I Thessalonians 4:12)

9. Why do we always seem to want to accumulate more?

"A feast is made for laughter, and wine maketh merry: but money answereth all things."

A party gives giggling, and wine gives happiness, and money gives everything!

In general, people think money is the response to every problem.

(Ecclesiastes 10:19)

"And when he was gone forth into the way, there came one running, and kneeled to him, and asked him, Good Master, what shall I do that I may inherit eternal life?"

"And Jesus said unto him, Why callest thou me good? There is none good but one, that is, God."

"Thou knowest the commandments, DO NOT COMMIT ADULTERY, DO NOT KILL DO NOT STEAL, DO NOT BEAR FALSE WITNESS, Defraud not, HONOUR THY FATHER, AND MOTHER."

"And he answered and said unto him, Master, all these have I observed from my youth."

"Then Jesus beholding him loved him, and said unto him, One thing thou lackest: go thy way, sell whatsoever thou hast, and give to the poor, and thou shalt have treasure in heaven: and come, take up the cross, and follow me."

"And he was sad at that saying, and went away grieved: for he had great possessions."

"And Jesus looked round about, and saith unto his disciples, How hardly shall they that have riches enter into the kingdom of God!"

We accumulate money since we trust money and riches to bring us happiness. The much happier and gainful we could be on the if we set our minds on accumulating treasure in heaven.

(Mark 10:17-23)

10. Why don't I ever seem to have enough?

"Ho, every one that thirsteth, come ye to the waters, and he that hath no money; come ye, buy, and eat; yea, come, buy wine and milk without money and without price."

Wherefore do ye spend money for that which is not bread? And your labour for that which satisifieth not? Hearken diligently unto me, and eat ye that which is good, and let your soul delight itself in fatness."

Why spend your money on food that does not give you strength?…

Because we foolishly spend our money on what doesn't fulfill or satisfy the soul.

(Isaiah 55:1, 2)

"Then came the word of the LORD by Hag'-gai the prophet, saying,"

"Is it time for you, O ye, to dwell in your cielded houses, and this house lie in waste?"

"Now therefore thus saith the LORD of hosts: Consider your ways."

"Ye have sown much, and bring in little; ye eat, but ye have not enough; ye drink, but ye are not filled with drink; ye clothe you, but there is none warm; and he that earneth wages earneth wages to put it into a bag with holes."

We do not manage our money according to God's priorities.

(Haggai 1:3-6)

"And one of the company said unto him, Master, speak to my brother, that he divide the inheritance with me."

"And he said unto him, Man, who made me a judge or a divider over you?"

"And he said unto them, Take heed, and beware of covetousness: for a man's life consisteth not in the abundance of the things which he possesseth.

"And he spake a parable unto them, saying, The ground of a certain rich man brought forth plentifully:"

"And he thought within himself, saying, What shall I do, because I have no room where to bestow my fruits?"

"And he said, This will I do: I will pull down my barns, and build greater; and there will I bestow all my fruits and my goods."

"And I will say to my soul, Soul, thou hast much goods laid up for many years; take thine ease, eat, drink, and be merry."

"But God said unto him, Thou fool, this night thy soul shall be required of thee: then whose shall those things be, which thou hast provided?"

"So is he that layeth up treasure for himself, and is not rich toward God."

Do not to be avaricious (greedy) for what you don't have. Life isn't measured by the amount we possess (by what we have).

If we rely upon our riches (wealth) to bring security, there will never be enough.

(Luke 12:13-21)

11. Is debt a sin?

"Then came Peter to him, and said, Lord, how oft shall my brother sin against me, and I forgive him? till seven times?"

"Jesus saith unto him, I say not unto thee, Until seven times: but, Until seventy times seven."

"Therefore is the kingdom of heaven likened unto a certain king, which would take account of his servants."

"And when he had begun to reckon, one was brought unto him, which owed him ten thousand talents."

"But forasmuch as he had not to pay, his lord commanded him to be sold, and his wife, and children, and all that he had, and payment to be made."

"The servant therefore fell down, and worshipped him, saying, Lord, have patience with me, and I will pay thee all."

"Then the lord of that servant was moved with compassion, and loosed him, and forgave him the debt."

"But the same servant went out, and found one of his fellowservants, which owed him an hundred pence: and he laid hands on him, and took him by the throat, saying, Pay me that thou owest."

"And his fellowservant fell down at his feet, and besought him, saying, Have patience with me, and I will pay thee all."

"And he would not; but went and cast him into prison, till he should pay the debt."

"So when his fellowservants saw what was done, they were very sorry, and came and told unto their lord all that was done."

"Then his lord, after that he had called him, said unto him, O thou wicked servant, I forgave thee all that debt, because thou desiredst me:"

"Shouldest not thou also have had compassion on thy fellowservant, even as I had pity on thee?"

"And his lord was wroth, and delivered him to the tormentors, till he should pay all that was due unto him."

All the while, one of his account holders was acquired who owed him a great many dollars.

The teaching on forgiveness, Jesus uses this story that appears to expect the loaning or borrowing of money isn't itself evil, however the way where we respond to obligations can be.

(Matthew 18:21-35)

"The rich ruleth over the poor, and the borrower is servant to the lender."

In spite of the fact that borrowing money isn't, in itself, sinful, we are to be cautious and wise in our borrowing so we don't become slaves to debt.

(Proverbs 22:7)

"MY son, if thou be surety for thy friend, if thou hast stricken thy hand with a stranger,"

"Thou art snared with the words of thy mouth, thou art taken with the words of thy mouth."

"So this now, my son, and deliver thyself, when thou art come into the hand of thy friend; go, humble thyself, and make sure thy friend."

"Give not sleep as a roe from the hand of the hunter, and as a bird from the hand of the fowler."

If you co-sign a loan for a friend or guarantee the debt of someone you hardly know…

get out of it if you possibly can!

Debt isn't a sin, but it is a perilous thing. We are to keep away from it at whatever point possible.

(Proverbs 6:1-5)

"Owe no man any thing, but to love one another: for he that loveth another hath fulfilled the law."

In spite of the fact that bringing about debt may not be sinful, the inability to reimburse (repay) a debt is.

(Romans 13:8)

PROMISE FROM GOD

"Therefore take no thought, saying, What shall we eat? or, What shall we drink? Or, Wherewithal shall we be clothed?"

"(For after all these things do the Gentiles seek:) for your heavenly Father knoweth that ye have need of all these things."

"But seek ye first the kingdom of God, and his righteousness; and all these things shall be added unto you."

So don't stress over having enough food or drink or apparel. Why resemble the pagans who are so profoundly worried about these things? Your heavenly Father already knows every one of your needs, and he will provide all of you needs from everyday that you live for him and make the Kingdom of God your primary concern.

(Matthew 6:31-33)

MOTIVES

12. So long as we do the right thing, what difference does our motive make?

"And in process of time it came to pass, that Cain brought of the fruit of the ground an offering unto the LORD."

"And Abel, he also broought of the firstlings of his flock and of the fat thereof. And the LORD had respect unto Abel and to his offering:"

"But unto Cain and to his offering he had not respect. And Cain was very wroth, and his countenance fell."

All things considered, Cain's sacrifice was viewed as wrong since his thought processes (motives) were tainted.

(Genesis 4:3-5)

"Take heed that ye do not your alms before men, to be seen of them: otherwise ye have no reward of your Father which is in heaven."

"Therefore when thou doest thine alms, do not sound a trumpet before thee, as the hypocrites do in the synagogues and in the streets, that they may have glory of men.

Verily I say unto you, They have their reward."

"But when thou doest alms, let not thy left hand know what thy right hand doeth:"

"That thine alms may be in secret: and thy Father which seeth in secret himself shall reward thee openly."

"And when thou prayest, thou shalt not be as the hypocrites are: for they love to pray standing in the synagogues and in the corners of the streets, that they may be seen of men. Verily I say unto you, They have their reward."

"But thou, when thou prayest, enter into thy closet, and when thou hast shut thy door, pray to the Father which is in secret; and thy Father which seeth in secret shall reward thee openly."

"But when ye pray, use not vain repetitions, as the heathen do: for they think that they shall be heard for their much speaking."

"Be not ye therefore like unto them: for your Father knoweth what things ye have need of, before ye ask him."

"And Simon Peter answered and said, Thou art the Christ, the Son of the living God."

"And Jesus answered and said unto him, Blessed art thou, Simon Bar-jo'-na; for flesh and blood hath not revealed it unto thee, but my Father which is in heaven."

"And I say also unto thee, That thou art Peter, and upon this rock I will build my church;

and the gates of hell shall not prevail against it."

Do not to carry out your good deeds openly, to be admired, in light of the fact that then you will lose the reward from your Father in heaven.

When we seek after spiritual life with self-serving intentions (self-serving motives), we deny (rob) ourselves of the joy God intends.

(Matthew 6:1-8, 16-18)

"What then? Notwithstanding, every way, whether in pretense, or in truth, Christ is preached; and I therein do rejoice, yea, and will rejoice."

(Philippians 1:18)

13. How can I have purer motives?

"Now therefore, in the sight of all Israel the congregation of the LORD, and in the audience of our God, keep and seek for all the commandments of the LORD your God: that ye may possess this good land, and leave it for an inheritance for your children after you for ever."

"And thou, Solomon my son, know thou the God of thy father, and serve him with a perfect heart and with a willing mind: for the LORD searcheth all hearts, and understandeth all the imaginations of the thoughts: if thou seek him, he will be found of thee; but if thou forsake him, he will cast thee off for ever."

"Take heed now; for the LORD hath chosen thee to build an house for the sanctuary; be strong, and do it."

We must learn to serve the Lord with a pure heart and mind.

(I Chronicles 28:8-10)

"Every way of a man is right in his own eyes: but the LORD pondereth the hearts."

People may think they are making the wisest decision, but the LORD analyzes the heart. We should perceive that God is as keen on thought process (motives) as he is in deed.

(Proverbs 21:2)

"Let a man so account of us, as of the ministers of Christ, and stewards of the mysteries of God."

"Moreover it is required in stewards, that a man be found faithful."

"But with me it is a very small thing that I should be judged of you, or of man's judgment: yea, I judge not mine own self."

"For I know nothing by myself; yet am I not hereby justified: but he that judgeth me is the Lord."

"Therefore judge nothing before the time, until the Lord come, who both will bring to light the hidden things of darkness, and will make manifest the counsels of the hearts:

and then shall every man have praise of God."

My conscience is unmistakably clear, however that isn't what is important. It is simply the Lord who will look at me and decide...

Remember that God alone knows your heart. Request that he reveal to you any area wherein your motives are less than pure.

(I Corinthians 4:1-5)

PROMISE FROM GOD

"A new heart also will I give you, and a new spirit will I put within you: and I will take away the stony heart out of your flesh, and I will give you an heart of flesh."

And I will give you a new heart with new and right desires, and I will put a new spirit in you. I will take out your stony hearts of sin and give you new, obedient hearts.

(Ezekiel 36:26)

NEGLECT

14. What can I do when I feel neglected?

"Blessed be God, which hath not turned away my prayer, nor his mercy from me."

While others may neglect us, God never turns away from us.

(Psalm 66:20)

"Sing unto God, sing praises to his name: extol him that rideth upon the heavens by his name JAH, and rejoice before him."

"A father of the fatherless, and a judge of the widows, is God in his holy habitation."

"God setteth the solitary in families: he bringeth out those which are bound with chains:

but the rebellious dwell in a dry land."

Rejoice in the continuous presence of our Lord.

(Psalm 68:4-6)

"Draw nigh to God, and he will draw nigh to you. Cleanse your hands, ye sinners; and purify your hearts, ye double minded."

Draw close to God, and God will draw close to you.

When we feel neglected we must not let these feelings cause us to withdraw from God.

(James 4:8)

15. What are the signs of neglect? How do I know when I am neglecting someone?

"What doth it profit, my brethren, though a man say he hath faith, and have not works?

can faith save him?

Dear Brothers and sisters, what's the use of saying you have faith if you don't demonstrate it (of you don't show it) by your actions? That kind of faith can't save anybody. If you are not successfully helping other people or serving in your congregation, you are being careless, neglectful.

(James 2:14)

"Woe unto you, scribes and Pharisees, hypocrites! for ye pay tithe of mint and aanise and cummin, and have omitted the weightier matters of the law, judgment, mercy, and faith: these ought ye to have done, and not to leave the other undone."

But you ignore important things of the law-justice, mercy, and faith.

Ask yourself, and others, if you are neglecting what is truly important.

(Matthew 23:23)

16. How can I prevent neglect?

"Train up a child in the way he should go: and when he is old, he will not depart from it."

Diligently teach your children the truths of the Bible.

(Proverbs 22:6)

"LET brotherly love continue."

"Be not forgetful to entertain strangers: for thereby some have entertained angels unawares."

"Remember them that are in bonds, as bound with them; and them which suffer adversity, as being yourselves also in the body."

Don't forget to show hospitality to strangers...Share the sorrow of those being mistreated...

(Hebrews 13:1-3)

"When the Son of man shall come in his glory, and all the holy angels with him, then shall he sit upon the throne of his glory:"

"And before him shall be gathered all nations: and he shall separate them one from another, as a shepherd divideth his sheep from the goats:"

"And he shall set the sheep on his right hand, but the goats on the left."

"Then shall the King say unto them on his right hand, Come, ye blessed of my Father, inherit the kingdom prepared for you from the foundation of the world:"

"For I was an hungred, and ye gave me meat: I was thristy, and ye gave me drink: I was a stranger, and ye took me in:"

"Naked, and ye clothed me: I was sick, and ye visited me: I was in prison, and ye came unto me."

'Then shall the righteous answer him, saying, Lord, when saw we thee an hungred, and fed thee? or thirsty, and gave thee drink?"

"When saw we thee a stranger, and took thee in? or naked, and clothed thee?"

"Or when saw we thee sick, or in prison, and came unto thee?"

"And the King shall answer and say unto them, Verily I say unto you, Inasmuch as ye have done it unto one of the least of these my brethren, ye have done it unto me."

"Then shall he say also unto them on the left hand, Depart from me, ye cursed, into everlasting fire, prepared for the devil and his angels:"

"For I was hungred, and ye gave me no meat: I was thirsty, and ye gave me no drink:"

"I was a stranger, and ye took me not in: naked, and ye clothed me not: sick, and in prison, and ye visited me not."

Then shall they also answer him, saying, Lord, when saw we thee an hungred, or athirst, or a stranger, or naked, or sick, or in prison, and did not minister unto thee?"

"Then shall he answer them, saying, Verily I say unto you, Inasmuch as ye did it not to one of the least of these, ye did it not to me."

"And these shall go away into everlasting punishment: but the righteous into life eternal."

There are such a large number of people in need; move in to help those people who are longing for it.

(Matthew 25:31-46)

17. How do we neglect God?

"Then contended I with the rulers, and said, Why is the house of God forsaken? And I gathered them together, and set them in their place."

Why has the Temple of God been neglected? Then I called all the Levites back again and restored them to their proper duties."

(Nehemiah 13:11)

"Not forsaking the assembling of ourselves together, as the manner of some is; but exhorting one another; and so much the more, as ye see the day approaching."

And let us not neglect our meeting together, as some people do, but encourage and warn each other."

We neglect God when we neglect the church and our responsibility to serve within it.

(Hebrews 10:25)

"And every one that heareth these sayings of mine, and doeth them not, shall be likened unto a foolish man, which built his house upon the sand:"

Anyone who hears my teaching and ignores it is foolish, like a person who builds a house on sand.

(Matthew 7:26)

"THEREFORE we ought to give the more earnest heed to the things which we have heard, lest at any time we should let them slip."

(Hebrews 2:1)

"That his heart be not lifted up above his brethren, and that he turn not aside from the commandment, to the right hand, or to the left: to the end that he may prolong his days in his kingdom, he, and his children, in the midst of Israel."

This regular reading will prevent him from...turning away from these commands in the smallest way..."

We neglect God when we ignore the Bible.

(Deuteronomy 17:20)

"How shall we escape, if we neglect so great salvation; which at the first began to be spoken by the Lord, and was confirmed unto us by them that heard him;"

What makes us think we can escape if we are indifferent to this great salvation that was announced by the Lord Jesus himself?

(Hebrews 2:3)

"Be not deceived; God is not mocked: for whatsoeveer a man soweth, that shall he also reap."

We neglect God when we ignore his offer of salvation.

(Galatians 6:7)

"Therefore to him that knoweth to do good, and doeth it not, to him it is sin."

Remember, it is sin to know what you ought to do and then not do it.

We neglect God when we ignore what we know is right.

(James 4:17)

PROMISE FROM GOD

"Looking diligently lest any man fail of the grace of God; lest any root of bitterness springing up trouble you, and thereby many be defiled;"

Look after each other so that none of you will miss out on the special favor of God.

(Hebrews 12:15)

OBEDIENCE

18. Obedience seems like such an authoritarian concept. Does God really require absolute obedience?

"NOW these are the commandments, the statutes, and the judgments, which the LORD your God commanded to teach you, that ye might do them in the land whither ye go to possess it:"

"That thou mightest fear the LORD thy God, to keep all the statutes and his commandments, which I command thee, thou, and thy son, and thy son's son, all the days of thy life; and that thy days may be prolonged."

"Hear therefore, O Israel, and observe to do it; that it may be well with thee, and that ye may increase mightily; as the LORD God of thy fathers hath promised thee, in the land that floweth with milk and honey."

"Hear, O Israel: The LORD our God is one LORD:"

"And thou shalt love the LORD thy God with all thine heart, and with all thy soul, and with all thy might."

"And these words, which I command thee this day, shall be in thine heart:"

"And thou shalt teach them diligently unto thy children, and shalt talk of them when thou sittest in thine house, and when thou walkest by the way, and when thou liest down, and when thou risest up."

"And thou shalt bind them all for a sign upon thine hand, and they shall be as frontlets between thine eyes."

"And thou shalt write them upon the posts of thy house, and on thy gates."

"And it shall be, when the LORD thy God shall have brought thee into the land which he sware unto thy fathers, to Abraham, to Isaac, and to Jacob, to give thee great and goodly cities, which thou buildest not,"

"And houses full of all good things, which thou diggedsst not, vineyards and olive trees, which thou plantedst not; when thou shalt have eaten and be full;"

"Then beware lest thou forget the LORD, which brought thee forth out of the land of Egypt, from the house of bondage."

"Thou shalt fear the LORD thy God, and serve him, and shalt swear by his name."

"Ye shall not go after other gods, of the gods of the people which are round about you;"

"(For the LORD thy God is a jealous God among you) lest the anger of the LORD thy God be kindled against thee, and destroy thee from off the face of the earth."

"Ye shall not tempt the LORD your God, as ye tempteed him in Mas'-sah."

"Ye shall diligently keep the commandments of the LORD your God, and his testimonies, and his statutes, which he hath commanded thee."

"And thou shalt do that which is right and good in the sight of the LORD: that it may be well with thee, and that thou mayest go in and possess the good land which the LORD sware unto thy fathers,"

"Ton cast out all thine enemies from before thee, as the LORD hath spoken."

"And when thy son asketh thee in time to come, saying, What mean the testimonies, and statutes, and the judgments, which the LORD our God hath commanded you?"

"Then thou shalt say unto thy son, We were Pharaoh's bondmen in Egypt; and the LORD brought us out of Egypt with a mighty hand:"

"And the LORD shewed signs and wonders, great and sore, upon Egypt, upon Pharaoh, and upon all his household, before our eyes:"

"And he brought us out from thence, that he might bring us in, to give us the land which he sware unto our fathers."

"And the LORD commanded us to do all these statutes, to fear the LORD our God, for our good always, that he might preserves us alive, as it is at this day."

"And it shall be our righteousness, if we observe to do all these commandments before the LORD our God, as he hath commanded us."

(Deuteronomy 6:1-25)

"Behold, I set before you this day a blessing and a curse;"

"A blessing, if ye obey the commandments of the LORD your God, which I command you this day:"

"And a curse, if ye will not obey the commandments of the LORD your God, but turn aside out of the way which I command you this day, to go after other gods, which ye have not known."

(Deuteronomy 11:26-28)

"AND it shall come to pass, if thou shalt hearken diligently unto the voice of the LORD thy God, to observe and to do all his commandments which I command thee this day, that the LORD thy God will set thee on high above all nations of the earth:"

"And all these blessings shall come on thee, and overtake thee, if thou shalt hearken unto the voice of the LORD thy God."

"Blessed shalt thou be in the city, and blessed shalt thou be in the field."

"Blessed shall be the fruit of thy body, and the fruit of thy ground, and the fruit of thy cattle, the increase of thy kine, and the flocks of thy sheep."

"Blessed shall be thy basket and thy store."

"Blessed shalt thou be when thou comest in, and blessed shalt thou be when thou goest out."

"The LORD shall cause thine enemies that rise up against thee to he smitten before thy face: they shall come out against thee one way, and flee before thee seven ways."

"The LORD shall command the blessing upon thee in thy storehouses, and in all that thou settest thine hand unto; and he shall bless thee in the land which the LORD thy God giveth thee."

"The LORD shall establish thee an holy people unto himself, as he hath sworn unto thee, if thou shalt keep the commandments of the LORD thy God, and walk in his ways."

"And all the people of the earth shall that thou art called by the name of the LORD; and they shall be afraid of thee."

"And the LORD shall make thee plenteous in goods, in the fruit of thy body, and in the fruit of thy cattle, and in the fruit of thy ground, in the land which the LORD sware unto thy fathers to give thee."

"The LORD shall open unto thee his good treasure, the heaven to give the rain unto thy land in his season, and to bless all the work of thine hand: and thou shalt lend unto many nations, and thou shalt not borrow."

"And the LORD shall make thee the head, and not the tail; and thou shalt be above only;

and thou shalt not be beneath; if that thou hearken unto the commandments of the LORD thy God, which I command thee this day, to observe and to do them:"

"And thou shalt not go aside from any of the words which I command thee this day, to the right hand, or to the left, to go after other gods to serve them."

"But it shall come to pass, if thou wilt not hearken unto the voice of the LORD thy God, to observe to do all his commandments and his statutes which I command thee this day;

that all these curses shall come upon thee, and overtake thee:"

"Cursed shalt thou be in the city, and cursed shalt thou be in the field."

"Cursed shall be thy basket and thy store."

"Cursed shall be the fruit of thy body, and the fruit of thy land, the increase of thy kine, and the flocks of thy sheep."

"Cursed shalt thou be when thou comest in, and cursed shalt thou be when thou goest out."

"The LORD shall send upon thee cursing, vexation, and rebuke, in all that thou settest thine hand unto for to do, until thou be destroyed, and until thou perish quickly; because of the wickedness of thy doings, whereby thou hast forsaken me."

"The LORD shall make the pestilence cleave unto thee, until he have consumed thee from off the land, whither thou goest to possess it."

"The LORD shall smite thee with a consumption, and with a fever, and with an inflammation, and with an extreme burning, and with the sword, and with blasting, and with mildew; and they shall pursue thee until thou perish."

"And thy heaven that is over thy head shall be brass, and the earth that is under thee shall be iron."

"The LORD shall make the rain of thy land powder and dust: from heaven shall it come down upon thee, until thou be destroyed."

"The LORD shall cause thee to be smitten before thine enemies: thou shalt go out one way against them, and flee seven ways before them: and shalt be removed into all the kingdoms of the earth."

"And thy carcase shall be meat unto all fowls of the air, and unto the beasts of the earth, and no man shall fray them away."

"The LORD will smite thee with the botch of Egypt, and with the emerods, and with the scab, and with the itch, whereof thou canst not be healed."

"The LORD shall smite thee with madness, and blindness, and astonishment of heart:"

"And thou shalt grope at noonday, as the blind gropeth in darkness, and thou shalt not prosper in thy ways: and thou shalt be only oppressed and spoiled evermore, and no man shall save thee."

"Thou shalt betroth a wife, and another man shall lie with her: thou shalt build an house, and thou shalt not dwell therein: thou shalt plant a vineyard, and shalt not gather the grapes thereof."

"Thine ox shall be slain before thine eyes, and thou shalt not eat thereof: thine ass shall be violently taken away from before thy face, and shall not be restored to thee: thy sheep shall be given unto thine enemies, and thou shalt have none to rescue them."

"Thy sons and thy daughters shall be given unto another people, and thine eyes shall look, and fail with longing for them all the day long: and there shall be no might in thine hand."

"The fruit of thy land, and all thy labours, shall a nation which thou knowest not eat up;

and thou shalt be only oppressed and crushed always:"

"So that thou shalt be mad for the sight of thine eyes which thou shalt see."

"The LORD shall smite thee in the knees, and in the legs, with a sore botch that cannot be healed, from the sole of thy foot unto the top of thy head."

"The LORD shall bring thee, and thy king which thou shalt set over thee, unto a nation which neither thou nor thy fathers have known; and there shalt thou serve other gods, wood and stone."

"And thou shalt become an astonishment, a proverb, and a byword, among the nations whither the LORD shall lead thee."

"Thou shalt carry much seed out into the field, and shalt gather but little in; for the locust shall consume it."

"Thou shalt plant vineyards, and dress them, but shalt neither drink of the wine, nor gather the grapes; for the worms shall eat them.'

"Thou shalt have olive trees throughout all thy coasts, but thou shalt not anoint thyself with the oil; for thine olive shall cast his fruit."

"Thou shalt beget sons and daughters, but thou shalt not enjoy them; for they shall go into captivity."

"All thy trees and fruit of thy land shall the locust consume."

"The stranger that is within shall get up above thee very high; and thou shalt come down very low."

"He shall lend to thee, and thou shalt not lend to him: he shall be the head, and thou shalt be the tail."

"Moreover all these curses shall come upon thee, and shall pursue thee, and overtake thee, till thou be destroyed; because thou hearkenedst not unto the voice of the LORD thy God, to keep his commandments and his statutes which he commanded thee:"

"And they shall be upon thee for a sign and for a wonder, and upon thy seed for ever."

"Because thou servedst not the LORD thy God with joyfulness, and with gladness of heart, for the abundance of all things;"

"Therefore shalt thou serve thine enemies which the LORD shall send against thee, in hunger, and in thirst, and in nakedness, and in want of all things:

and he shall put a yoke of iron upon thy neck, until he have destroyed thee."

"The LORD shall bring a nation against thee from afar, from the end of the earth, as swift as the eagle flieth; a nation whose tongue thou shalt not understand;"

"A nation of fierce countenance, which shall not regard the person of the old, nor shew favour to the young:"

"And he shall eat the fruit of thy cattle, and the fruit of thy land, until thou be destroyed: which also shall not leave thee either corn, wine, or oil, or the increase of thy kine, or flocks of thy sheep, until he have destroyed thee."

"And he shall besiege thee in all thy gates, until thy high and fenced walls come down, wherein thou trustedst, throughout all thy land: and he shall besiege thee in all thy gates throughout all thy land, which the LORD thy God hath given thee."

"And thou shalt eat the fruit of thine own body, the flesh of thy sons and of thy daughters, which the LORD thy God hath given thee, in the siege, and in the straitness, wherewith thine enemies shall distress thee:"

"So that the man that is tender among you, and very delicate, his eye shall be evil toward his brother, and toward the wife of his bosom, and toward the remnant of his children which he shall leave:"

"So that he will not give to any of them of the flesh of his children whom he shall eat: because he hath nothing left him in the siege, and in the straitness, wherewith thine enemies shall distress thee in all thy gates."

"The tender and delicate woman among you, which would not adventure to set the sole of her foot upon the ground for delicateness and tenderness, her eye shall be evil toward her son, and toward her daughter,"

"And toward her young one that cometh out from between her feet, and toward her children which she shall bear: for she shall eat them for want of all things secretly in the siege and straitness, wherewith thine enemy shall distress thee in thy gates."

"If thou wilt not observe to do all the words of this law that are written in this book, that thou mayest fear this glorious and fearful name, THE LORD THY GOD;"

"Then the LORD will make thy plagues wonderful, and the plagues of thy seed, even great plagues, and of long continuance, and sore sicknesses, and of long continuance."

"Moreover he will bring upon thee all the diseases of Egypt, which thou wast afraid of;

and they shall cleave unto thee."

"Also every sickness, and every plague, which is not written in the book of this law, them will the LORD bring upon thee, until thou be destroyed."

"And ye shall be left few in number, whereas ye were as the stars of heaven for multitude; because thou wouldest not obey the voice of the LORD thy God."

"And it shall come to pass, that as the LORD rejoiced over you to do you good, and to multiply you; so the LORD will rejoice over you to destroy you, and to bring you to nought; and ye shall be plucked from off the land whither thou goest to possess it."

"And the LORD shall scatter thee among all people, from the one end of the earth even unto the other; and there thou shalt serve other gods, which neither thou nor thy fathers have known, even wood and stone."

"And among these nations shalt thou find no ease, neither shall the sole of thy foot have rest: but the LORD shall give thee there a trembling heart, and failing of eyes, and sorrow of mind:"

"And thy life shall hang in doubt before thee; and thou shalt fear day and night, and shalt have none assurance of thy life:"

"In the morning thou shalt say, Would God it were even! and at even thou shalt say, Would God it were morning! for the fear of thine heart wherewith thou shalt fear, and for the sight of thine eyes which thou shalt see."

"And the LORD shall bring thee into Egypt again with ships, by the way whereof I spake unto thee, Thou shalt see it no more again: and there ye shall be sold unto your enemies for bondmen and bondwomen, and no man shall buy you."

These passages of scripture demonstrate clearly that God's demand for obedience is based on his commitment to our well-being.

(Deuteronomy 28:1-68)

"THEN came the children of Israel, even the whole congregation, into the desert of Zin in the first month:

and the people abode in Ka'-desh; and Miriam died there, and was buried there."

"And there was no water for the congregation: and they gathered themselves together against Moses and against Aaron."

"And the people chode with Moses, and spake, saying, Would God that we had died when our brethren died before the LORD!"

"And why have ye brought up the congregation of the LORD into this wilderness, that we and our cattle should die there?"

"And wherefore have ye made us to come up out of Egypt, to bring us in unto this evil place? It is no place of seed, or of figs, or of vines, or of pomegranates; neither is there any water to drink."

"And Moses and Aaron went from the presence of the assembly unto the door of the tabernacle of the congregation, and they fell upon their faces: and the glory of the LORD appeared unto them."

"And the LORD spake unto Moses, saying,"

"Take the rod, and gather thou the assembly together, thou, and Aaron thy brother, and speak ye unto the rock before their eyes; and it shall give forth his water, and thou shalt bring forth to them water out of the rock: so thou shalt give the congregation and their beasts drink."

"And Moses took the rod from before the LORD, as he commanded him."

"And Moses and Aaron gathered the congregation together before the rock, and he said unto them, Hear now, ye rebels; must we fetch you water out of this rock?"

"And Moses lifted up his hand, and with his rod he smote the rock twice: and the water came out abundantly, and the congregation drank, and their beasts also."

"And the LORD spake unto Moses and Aaron, Because ye believed me not, to sanctify me in the eyes of the children of Israel, therefore ye shall not bring this congregation into the land which I have given them."

"This is the water of Mer'-i-bah; because the children of Israel strove with the LORD, and he was sanctified in them."

Disobedience always brings negative consequences, even for a spiritual leader.

(Numbers 20:1-13)

'Let no man deceive you with vain words: for because of these things cometh the wrath of God upon the children of disobedience."

Disobedience is sin and always lead to separation from God.

(Ephesians 5:6)

"Let this mind be in you, which was also in Christ Jesus:"

"Who, being in the form of God, thought it not robbery to be equal with God:"

"But made himself of no reputation, and took upon him the form of a servant, and was made in the likeness of men:"

"And being found in fashion as a man, he humbled himself, and became obedient unto death, even the death of the cross."

"Wherefore God also hath highly exalted him, and given him a name which is above every name:"

"That at the name of Jesus every knee should bow, of things in heaven, and things in earth, and things under the earth;"

"And that every tongue should confess that Jesus Christ is Lord, to the glory of God the Father."

"Where, my beloved, as ye have always obeyed, not as in my presence only, but now much more in my absence, work out your own salvation with fear and trembling."

"For it is God which worketh in you both to will and to do of his good pleasure."

Though he was God, he did not demand and cling to his rights as God...he obediently humbled himself...

(Philippians 2:5-13)

"Who in the days of his flesh, when he had offered up prayers and supplications with strong crying and tears unto him that was able to save him from death, and was heard in that he feared;"

"Though he were a Son, yet learned he obedience by the things which he suffered;"

"And being made perfect, he became the author of eternal salvation unto all them that obey him;"

Jesus is our example for obedience, even when obedience means suffering.

(Hebrews 5:7-9)

19. Does obedience to God get me into heaven?

"Knowing that a man is not justified by the works of the law, but by the faith of Jesus Christ, even we have believed in Jesus Christ, that we might be justified by the faith of Christ, and not by the works of the law: for by the works of the law shall no flesh be justified."

"But if, while we seek to be justified by Christ, we ourselves also are found sinners, is therefore Christ the minister of sin? God forbid."

"For if I build again the things which I destroyed, I make myself a transgressor."

"For I though the law am dead to the law, that I might live unto God."

"I am crucified with Christ: nevertheless I live; yet not I, but Christ liveth in me: and the life which I now live in the flesh I live by fai9[th] of the Son of God, who loved me, and gave himself for me."

I do not frustrate the grace of God: for if righteousness come by the law, then Christ is dead in vain."

Obedience to strict laws (religious laws) can never save us. Be that as it may, when we accept Jesus Christ, we are progressively motivated to obey God out of love for him.

(Galatians 2:16-21)

"If ye love me, keep my commandments."

"And I will pray the Father, and he shall give you another Comforter, that he may abide with you for ever;"

"He that hath my commandments, and keepeth them, he it is that loveth me: and he that loveth me shall be loved of my Father, and I will love him, and will manifest myself to him."

"Jusas saith unto him, not Is-car'-i-ot, Lord, how is it that thou wilt manifest thyself unto us, and not unto the world?"

"Jesus answered and said unto him, If a man love me, he will keep my words: and my Father will love him, and we will come unto him, and make our abode with him."

"He that loveth me not keepeth not my sayings: and the word which ye hear is not mine, but the Father's which sent me."

Obedience to Jesus Christ is to be an expression of love.

(John 14:15-16, 21-24)

"By faith Noah, being warned of God of things not seen as yet, moved with fear, prepared an ark to the saving of his house; by the which he condemned the world, and became heir of the righteousness which is by faith."

"By faith Abraham, when he was called to go out into a place which he should after receive for an inheritance, obeyed,; and he went out, not knowing whither he went."

"By faith he sojourned in the land of promise, as in a strange country, dwelling in tabernacles with Isaac and Jacob, the heirs with him of the same promise:"

"For he looked for a city which hath foundations, whose builder and maker is God."

These obeyed by faith because their obedience is anchored in faith.

(Hebrews 11:7-10)

20. What if I have lived a life of disobedience?

"But what think ye? A certain man had two sons; and he came to the first, and said, Son, go work to day in my vineyard."

"He answered and said, I will not; but afterward he repented, and went."

"And he came to the second, and said likewise. And he answered and said, I go, sir: and went not."

"Whether of them twain did the will of the father? They say unto him, The first. Jesus saith unto them, Verily I say unto you, That the publicans and the harlots go into the kingdom of God before you."

It is never too late to repent and obey God!

(Matthew 21:28-31)

PROMISE FROM GOD

"FOR THIS IS THE COVENANT THAT I WILL MAKE WITH THE HOUSE OF ISRAEL AFTER THOSE DAYS, SAITH THE LORD; I WILL PUT MY LAWS INTO THEIR MIND, AND WRITE THEM IN THEIR HEARTS; AND I WILL BE TO THEM A GOD, AND THEY SHALL BE TO ME A PEOPLE:"

(Hebrews 8:10)

OPPORTUNITIES

21. How do I know an opportunity is from God?

"Redeeming the time, because the days are evil."

Make the most of every opportunity for doing good in these evil days."

(Ephesians 5:16)

"And the angel of the Lord spake unto Philip, saying, Arise, and go toward the south unto the way that goeth down from Jerusalem unto Ga'-za, which is desert."

"And he arose and went: and, behold, a man of E-thi-o'-pi-a, an eunuch of great authority under Can-da'-ce queen of the E-thi-o'-pi-ans, who had charge of all her treasure, and had come to Jerusalem for to worship,"

"Was returning, and sitting in his chariot read E-sa'-ias the prophet."

"Then the Spirit said unto Philip, Go near, and join thyself to this chariot."

"And Philip ran thither to him, and heard him read the prophet E-sa'-ias, and said, Understandest thou what thou readest?"

"And he said, How can I, except some man should guide me? And he desired Philip that he would come up and sit with him."

"The place of the scripture which he read was this, HE WAS LED AS A SHEEP TO THE SLAUGHTER; AND LIKE A LAMB DUMB BEFORE HIS SHEARER, SO OPENED HE NOT HIS MOUTH:"

"IN HIS HUMILIATION HIS JUDGMENT WAS TAKEN AWAY: AND WHO SHALL DECLARE HIS GENERATION? FOR HIS LIFE IS TAKEN FROM THE EARTH."

"And the eunuch answered Philip, and said, I pray thee, of whom speaketh the prophet this? of himself, or of some other man?"

"Then Philip opened his mouth, and began at the same scripture, and preached unto him Jesus."

"And as they went on their way, they came unto a certain water: and the eunuch said, See, here is water; what doth hinder me to be baptized?"

"And Philip said, If thou believest with all thine heart, thou mayest. And he answered and said, I believe that Jesus Christ is the Son of God."

"And he commanded the chariot to stand still: and they went down both into the water, both Philip and the eunuch; and he baptized him."

We are consistently to be prepared to take advantage of an opportunity to witness for Christ.

(Acts 8:26-38)

"But I would ye should understand, brethren, that the things which happened unto me have fallen not rather unto the furtherance of he gospel;"

"So that my bonds in Christ are manifest in all the palace, and in all other places;"

"And many of the brethren in the Lord, waxing confident by my bonds, are much more bold to speak the word without fear."

Furthermore, I need you to know, dear companions, that everything that has transpired here has helped with spreading the Good News.

Jesus Christ helps us turn our problems into opportunities.

(Philippians 1:12-14)

"Then shall the kingdom of heaven be likened unto ten virgins, which took their lamps, and went forth to meet the bridegroom."

"And five of them were wise, and five were foolish."

"They that were foolish took their lamps, and took no oil with them:"

"But the wise took oil in their vessels with their lamps."

"While the bridegroom tarried, they all slumbered and slept."

"And at midnight there was a cry made, Behold, the bridegroom cometh; go ye out to meet him."

"Then all those virgins arose, and trimmed their lamps.'

"And the foolish said unto the wise, Give us of your oil; for our lamps are gone out."

"But the wise answered, saying, Not so; lest there be not enough for us and you: but go rather to them that sell, and buy for yourselves."

"And while they went to buy, the bridegroom came; and they that were ready went in with him to the marriage: and the door was shut."

"Afterward came also the other virgins, saying, Lord, Lord, open to us."

"But he answered and said, Verily I say unto you, I know you not."

"Watch therefore, for ye know neither the day nor the hour wherein the Son of man cometh."

We should never pass up on the opportunity of accepting the unconditional present (free gift) of salvation from God.

(Matthew 25:1-13)

"And I gathered them together to the river that runneth to A-ha'-va; and there abode we in tents three days: and I viewed the people, and the priests, and found there none of the sons of Levi."

We should seize any opportunity to use our gifts for God.

(Ezra 8:15)

"And when we departed from Ho'-reb, we went through all that great and terrible wilderness, which ye saw by the way of the mountain of the Am'-or-ites, as the LORD our God commanded us; and we came to Ka'-desh-bar'-ne-a."

"And I said unto you, Ye are come unto the mountain of the Am'-or-ites, which the LORD our God doth give unto us."

"Behold, the LORD thy God hath set the land before thee: go up and possess it, as the LORD God of thy fathers hath said unto thee; fear not, neither be discouraged."

"And ye came near unto me every one of you, and said, We will send men before us, and they shall search us out the land, and bring us word again by what way we must go up, and into what cities we shall come."

"And the saying pleased me well: and I took twelve men of you, one of a tribe:"

"And they turned and went up into the mountain, and came unto the valley of Esh'-col, and searched it out."

"And they took of the fruit of the land in their hands, and brought it down unto us, and brought us word again, and said, It is a good land which the LORD our God doth give us.

"Notwithstanding ye would not go up, but rebelled against the commandment of the LORD your God:"

"And ye murmured in your tents, and said, Because the LORD hated us, he hath brought us forth out of the land of Egypt, to deliver us into the hand of the Am'-or-ites, to destroy us."

"Whiter shall we go up? our brethren have discouraged our heart, saying, The people is greater and taller than we; the cities are great and walled up to heaven; and moreover we have seen the sons of the An'-a-kims there."

"Then I said unto you, Dread not, neither be afraid of them."

"The LORD your God which goeth before you, he shall fight for you, according to all that he did for you in Egypt before your eyes;"

Fear and Doubt can cause us to miss God's opportunities.

(Deuteronomy 1:19-30)

"For the kingdom of heaven is as a man travelling into a far country, who called his own servants, and delivered unto them his goods."

"And unto one he gave five talents, to another two, and to another one; to every man according to his several ability; and straightway took his journey."

"Then he that had received the five talents went and traded with the same, and made them other five talents."

"And likewise he that had received two, he also gained other two."

"But he that had received one went and digged in the earth, and hid his lord's money."

"After a long time the lord of those servants cometh, and reckoneth with them."

"And so he that had received five talents came and brought other five talents, saying, Lord, thou deliveredst unto me five talents: behold I have gained beside them five talents more."

"His lord said unto him, Well done, thou good and faithful servant: thou hast been faithful over a few things, I will make thee ruler over many things: enter thou into the joy of thy lord."

"He also that had received two talents came and said, Lord, thou deliveredst unto me two talents: behold, I have gained two other talents beside them."

"His lord said unto him, Well done, good and faithful servant; thou hast been faithful over a few things, I will make thee ruler over many things: enter thou into the joy of thy lord."

"Then he which had received the one talent came and said, Lord, I knew thee that thou art an hard man, reaping where thou hast not sown, and gathering where thou hast not strawed:"

"And I was afraid, and went and hid thy talent in the earth: lo, there thou hast that is thine."

"His lord answered and said unto him, Thou wicked and slothful servant, thou knewest that I reap where I sowed not, and gather where I have not strawed:"

"Thou oughtest therefore to have put my money to the exchangers, and then at my coming I should have received mine own with usury."

"Take thereforth the talent from him, and give it unto him which hath ten talents."

"For unto every one that hath shall be given, and he shall have abundance: but from him that hath not shall be taken away even that which he hath."

"And cast ye the unprofitable servant into outer darkness: there shall be weeping and gnashing of teeth."

God presents every one of us with ability and opportunity to contribute for the good and development (growth) of his Kingdom.

(Matthew 25:14-30)

PROMISE FROM GOD

"Walk in wisdom toward them that are without, redeeming the time."

Live wisely among those who are not Christians, and make the most of every opportunity.

(Colossians 4:5)

PARENTING

22. What does the Bible say about the role of parents?

"But continue thou in the things which thou hast learned and hast been assured of, knowing of whom thou hast learned them;"

"And that from a child thou hast known the holy scriptures, which are able to make thee wise unto salvation through faith which is in Christ Jesus."

You have been taught the holy Scriptures from childhood.

Parents are to assume liability for showing their youngsters a love for the Word of God.

(II Timothy 3:14, 15)

"Hear, O Israel: The Lord our God is one Lord:"

"And thou shalt love the LORD thy God with all thine heart and with all thy soul, and with all thy might."

"And these words, which I command thee this day, shall be in thine heart:"

"And thou shalt teach them diligently unto thy children, and shalt talk of them when thou sittest in thine house, and when thou walkest by the way, and when thou liest down, and when thou risest up."

"And thou shalt bind them for a sign upon thine hand, and they shall be as frontlets between thine eyes."

"And thou shalt write them upon the posts of thy house, and on they gates."

Repeat the scriptures again and again to your children.

Parents are responsibility not only to show their youngsters scriptural values but to demonstrate for them lives of obedience.

(Deuteronomy 6:4-9)

"My son, despise not the chastening of the LORD; neither be weary of his correction:"

"For whom the LORD loveth he correcteth; even as a father the son in whom he delighteth."

For the LORD corrects those he loves, similarly as a father corrects a child in whom he delights.

(Proverbs 3:11, 12)

'And ye have forgotten the exhortation which speaketh unto you as unto children, MY SON, DESPISE NOT THOU THE CHASTENING OF THE LORD, NOR FAINT WHEN THOU ART REBUKED OF HIM:"

"FOR WHOM THE LORD LOVETH HE CHASTENETH, AND SCOURGETH EVERY SON WHOM HE RECEIVETH."

"If ye endure chastening, God dealeth with you as with sons; for what son is he whom the father chasteneth not?"

"But if ye be without chastisement, whereof all are partakers, then are ye bastards, and not sons."

"Furthermore we have had fathers of our flesh which corrected us, and we gave them reverence: shall we not rather be in subjection unto the Father of spirits, and live?"

"For they verily for a few days chastened us after their own pleasure; but he for our profit, that we might be partakers of his holiness."

"Now no chastening for the present seemeth to be joyous, but grievous: nevertheless afterward it yieldeth the peaceable fruit of righteousness unto them which are exercised thereby."

No discipline is agreeable while it is going on it is agonizing! Be that as it may, subsequently there will be a calm reap (a quiet harvest) of right living...

Parents are to train their children with consistency, wisdon, and love.

(Hebrews 12:5-11)

"And Isaac loved Esau, because he did eat of his venison: but Rebekah loved Jacob."

Parents are not to show favoritism between children.

(Genesis 25:28)

"Wherefore kick ye at my sacrifice and at mine offering, which I have commanded in my habitation; and honourest thy sons above me, to make yourselves fat with the chiefest of all the offerings of Israel my people?"

Why do you honor your sons more than me?

Parents who are too liberal don't enable (help) their children to create (develop)

character.

(I Samuel 2:29)

"And when he came to himself, he said, How many hired servants of my father's have bread enough and to spare, and I perish with hunger!"

"I will arise and go to my father, and will say unto him, Father, I have sinned against heaven, and before thee."

"And am no more worthy to be called thy son: make me as one of thy hired servants."

"And he arose, and came to his father, But when he was yet a great way off, his father saw him, and had compassion, and ran, and fell on his neck, and kissed him."

"And the son said unto him, Father, I have sinned against heaven, and in thy sight, and am no more worthy to be called thy son."

"But the father said to his servants, Bring forth the best robe, and put it on him; and put a ring on his hand, and shoes on his feet:"

"For this my son was dead, and is alive again; he was lost, and is found, And they began to be merry."

Filled with love and compassion, he ran to his son, embraced him, and kissed him.

The hallmark of a living parent is the willingness to forgive.

(Luke 15:17-24)

23. How are children to relate to parents?

"Honour thy father and thy mother: that thy days may be long upon the land which the LORD thy God giveth thee."

(Exodus 20:12)

"Children, obey your parents in the Lord: for this is right."

"HONOUR THY FATHER AND MOTHER; which is the first commandment with promise;"

"THAT IT MAY BE WELL WITH THEE, AND THOU MAYEST LIVE LONG ON THE EARTH."

Children, obey your parents because you belong to the Lord.

(Ephesians 6:1-3)

24. What if I am a single parent or grew up in a single-parent home?

"But let the righteous be glad; let them rejoice before God: yea, let them exceedingly rejoice."

"Sing unto God, sing praises to his name: extol him that rideth upon the heavens by his name JAH, and rejoice before him."

"A father of the fatherless, and a judge of the widows, is God in his holy habitation."

"God setteth the solidary in families; he bringeth out those which are bound with chains:

but the rebellious dwell in a dry land."

God has a special place in his heart for those who are lonely or abandoned.

(Psalm 68:3-6)

PROMISE FROM GOD

"Train up a child in the way he should go: and when he is old, he will not depart from it."

(Proverbs 22:6)

PATIENCE

25. How can I grow in patience?

"And Moses returned unto the LORD, and said, Lord, wherefore hast thou so evil entreated this people? why is it that thou hast sent me?"

"For since I came to Pharaoh to speak in thy name, he hath done evil to this people;

neither hast thou delivered thy people at all."

We become fretful (impatient) when we center more around our plan than on God's will.

(Exodus 5:22, 23)

"I WAITED patiently for the LORD; and he incline unto me, and heard my cry."

We should stand by calmly in prayer for God to accomplish his work in us.

(Psalm 40:1)

"For the vision is yet for an appointed time, but at the end it shall speak, and not lie:

though it tarry, wait for it; because it will surely come, it will not tarry."

We develop patience as we learn to live from an eternal perspective.

(Habakkuk 2:3)

"But the fruit of the Spirit is love, joy, peace, longsuffering, gentleness, goodness, faith,"

Patience is a by-product of the presence and work of the Holy Spirit in our heart.

(Galatians 5:22)

"Charity suffereth long, and is kind; charity envieth not; charity vaunteth not itself, is not puffed up."

Love is patient and kind.

Patience is one of the evidences of love.

(I Corinthians 13:4)

"For we are saved by hope: but hope that is seen is not hope: for what a man seeth, why doth he yet hope for?"

"But if hope for that we see not, then do we with patience wait for it."

If we anticipate something we don't have yet, we should stand by patiently and confidently.

Patience is produced by the expectation (hope) a believer has in God's eternal glory.

(Romans 8:24, 25)

PROMISE FROM GOD

"The LORD is good unto them that wait for him, to the soul that seeketh him."

(Lamentations 3:25)

PEACE

26. Who is the true source of peace?

"I laid me down and slept; I awaked; for the LORD sustained me."

I laid down and slept. I woke up in security, for the LORD was watching over me.

(Psalm 3:5)

66

"I will both lay me down in peace, and sleep: for thou, LORD, only makest me dwell in safety."

(Psalm 4:8)

"The LORD will give strength unto his people; the LORD will bless his people with peace."

(Psalm 29:11)

"Thou art my hiding place; thou shalt preserve me from trouble; thou shalt compass me about with songs of deliverance."

(Psalm 32:7)

"And the peace of God, which passeth all understanding, shall keep your hearts and minds through Christ Jesus."

If you do this you will experience God's peace, which is unmistakably, wonderfully more great than the human mind can comprehend. His peace will watch your hearts and minds as you live in Christ Jesus.

True peace can't emerge out of non-serene, non-peaceful sources. God is the source of Peace. Try not to hope to find peace in a tempestuous world until you make peace with the God of Peace through Jesus Christ. Peace with God is finding peace with God, and that we can't do all alone, nor on our own. We must reconcile ourselves to God by asking that Jesus Christ forgive our sins and make us clean in God's sight.

(Philippians 4:7)

27. How can we get peace from God?

"Depart from evil, and thy lips from speaking guile."

Turn away from evil and do good. Work hard at living in peace with others.

Turn from sin to God.

(Psalm 34:14)

"Thou wilt keep him in perfect peace, whose mind is stayed on thee: because he trusteth in thee."

You will keep in perfect peace all who trust in you, whose considerations are fixed on you!

Trust in God to be with you in the entirety of your problems, and keep your thoughts on him.

(Isaiah 26:3)

"But the meek shall inherit the earth; and shall delight themselves in the abundance of peace."

The individuals who are gentle and humble will have the land; they will live in prosperous security.

Humble yourselves before the Lord.

(Psalm 37:11)

"Great peace have they which love thy law; and nothing shall offend them."

Those who love your law have peace and don't stumble. Love God's Word.

(Psalm 119:165)

"Glory to God in the highest, and on earth peace, good will toward men."

Always Please God!

(Luke 2:14)

"But the fruit of the Spirit is love, joy, peace, longsuffering, gentleness, goodness, faith,"

Cultivate the fruit of the Spirit in your life.

(Galatians 5:22)

"But glory, honour, and peace, every man that worketh good, to the Jew first, and also to the Gentile:"

Obey God.

(Romans 2:10)

28. How do we make peace with others?

"Finally, brethren, farewell. Be perfect, be of good comfort, be of one mind, live in peace; and the God of love and peace shall be with you."

Working hard at freeing sin from our own lives while perseveringly developing others accomplishes peace.

(II Corinthians 13:11)

"Endeavouring to keep the unity of the Spirit in the bond of peace."

Look for the unity that originates from the Holy Spirit.

(Ephesians 4:3)

"Recompense to no man evil for evil. Provide things honest in the sight of all men."

"If it be possible, as much as lieth in you, live peaceably with all men."

"Dearly beloved, avenge not yourselves, but rather give place unto wrath: for it is written, VENGEANCE IS MINE; I WILL REPAY, saith the Lord."

If you harbor sentiments of vengeance (revenge) in your heart, you can't find a sense of contentment (peace) with others.

(Romans 12:17-19)

"But the wisdom that is from above is first pure, then peaceable, gentle, and easy to be intreated, full of mercy and good fruits, without partiality, and without hypocrisy."

The wisdom that originates from heaven...is likewise peace loving, gentle consistently, and ready to respect (yield to) others. It is full of kindness (mercy) and great deeds. It shows no favoritism and is always sincere.

Commit yourselves to the good deeds that are the characteristic of a true peacemaker.

(James 3:17, 18)

PROMISE FROM GOD

"Peace I leave with you, my peace I give unto you: not as the world giveth, give I unto you. Let not your heart be troubled, neither let it be afraid."

(John 14:27)

PERSEVERANCE

29. How do I develop perseverance in my life?

"NOW Jericho was straitly shut up because of the children of Israel: none went out, and none came in."

"And the LORD said unto Joshua, See, I have given into thine hand Jericho, and the king thereof, and the mighty men of valour."

"And ye shall compass the city, all ye men of war, and go round about the city once.

Thus shalt thou do six days."

"And seven priests shall bear before the ark seven trumpets of rams' horns: and the seventh day ye shall compass the city seven times, and the priests shall blow with the trumpets."

"And it shall come to pass, that when they make a long blast with the ram's horn, and when ye hear the sound of the trumpet, all the people shall shout with a great shout; and the wall of the city shall fall down flat, and the people shall ascend up every man straight before him."

"And Joshua the son of Nun called the priests, and said unto them, Take up the ark of the covenant, and let seven priests bear seven trumpets of ram's horns before the ark of the LORD."

"AND he said unto the people, Pass on, and compass the city, and let him that is armed pass on before the ark of the LORD."

"And it came to pass, when Joshua had spoken unto the people, that the seven priests bearing the seven trumpets of rams' horns passed on before the LORD, and blew with the trumpets: and the ark of the covenant of the LORD followed them."

"And the armed men went before the priests that blew with the trumpets, and the rereward came after the ark, the priests going on, and blowing with the trumpets."

"And Joshua had commanded the people, saying, Ye shall not shout, nor make any noise with your voice, neither shall any word proceed out of your mouth, until the day I bid you shout; then shall ye shout."

"So the ark of the LORD compassed the city, going about it once; and they came into the camp, and lodged in the camp."

"And Joshua rose early in the morning, and the priests took up the ark of the LORD."

"And seven priests bearing seven trumpets of rams' horns before the ark of the LORD went on continually, and blew with the trumpets: and the armed men went before them; but the rereward came after the ark of the LORD, the priests going on, and blowing with the trumpets."

"And the second day they compassed the city once, and returned into the camp: so they did six days."

"And it came to pass on the seventh day, that they rose early about the dawning of the day, and compassed the city after the same manner seven times: only on that day they compassed the city seven times."

"And it came to pass at the seventh time, when the priests blew with the trumpets, Joshua said unto the people, Shout; for the LORD hath given you the city."

"And the city shall be accursed, even it, and all that are therein, to the LORD: only Ra'-hab the harlot shall live, she and all that are with her in the house, because she hid the messengers that we went."

"And ye, in any wise keep yourselves from the accursed thing, lest ye make yourselves accursed, when ye take of the accursed thing, and make the camp of Israel a curse, and trouble it."

"But all the silver, and gold, and vessels of brass and iron, are consecrated unto the LORD: they shall come into the treasury of the LORD."

"So the people shouted when the priests blew with the trumpets: and it came to pass, when the people heard the sound of the trumpet, and the people shouted with a great shout, that the wall fell down flat, so that the people went up into the city, every man straight before him, and they took the city."

Perseverance is obeying with in any event, even when God's way doesn't appear to make sense or produce results.

(Joshua 6:1-20)

"THEREFORE being justified by faith, we have peace with God through our Lord Jesus Christ:"

"By whom also we have access by faith into this grace wherein we stand, and rejoice in hope of the glory of God."

"And not only so, but we glory in tribulations also: knowing that tribulation worketh patience;"

"And patience, experience; and experience, hope:"

"And hope maketh not ashamed; because the love of God is shed abroad in our hearts by the Holy Ghost which is given unto us."

When we see the potential that suffering has to produce character in our lives, we continue on through it with God's help.

(Romans 5:1-5)

"Here is the patience of the saints: here are they that keep the commandments of God, and the faith of Jesus."

The key to perseverance for the believer is having a clear view of the goal of heaven.

(Revelation 14:12)

"And herein I give my advice: for this is expedient for you, who have begun before, not only to do, but also to be forward a year ago."

"Now therefore perform the doing of it; that as there was readiness to will, so there may be a performance also out of that which ye have."

I recommend that you finish what you began a year back, for you were the first to propose this thought, and ... the first to start taking care of business. Presently you should help this task through to culmination similarly as eagerly as you started it...

(II Corinthians 8:10, 11)

30. If we are saved by grace and not by works, where does perseverance come in?

"Take, my brethren, the prophets, who have spoken in the name of the Lord, for an example of suffering affliction, and of patience.'

"Behold, we count them happy which endure. Ye have heard of the patience of Job, and have seen the end of the Lord; that the Lord is very pitiful, and of tender mercy."

Perseverance in good works does not produce salvation. Rather, perseverance results from our faith in God.

(James 5:10, 11)

"And beside this, giving all diligence, add to your faith virtue; and to virtue knowledge;"

"And to knowledge temperance; and to temperance patience; and to patience godliness;"

"And to godliness brotherly kindness; and to brotherly kindness charity.'

"For if these things be in you, and abound, they make you that ye shall neither be barren nor unfruitful in the knowledge of our Lord Jesus Christ."

Patient endurance leads to godliness.

The Christian life begins with faith but grows through perseverance.

(II Peter 1:5-8)

"My brethren, count it all joy when ye fall into divers temptations;"

"Knowing this, that the trying of your faith worketh patience."

"But let patience have her perfect work, that ye may be perfect and entire, wanting nothing."

Perseverance is what turns suffering into maturity.

(James 1:2-4)

PROMISE FROM GOD

"For we are made partakers of Christ, if we hold the beginning of our confidence stedfast unto the end;"

(Hebrews 3:14)

PLANNING

31. Does God have a plan, or is everything just happening by chance?

"And Joseph said unto his brethren, Come near to me, I pray you. And they came near.

And he said, I am Joseph your brother, whom ye sold into Egypt."

"Now therefore be not grieved, nor angry with yourselves, that ye sold me hither: for God did send me before you to preserve life."

"For these two years hath the famine been in the land: and yet there are five yeas, in the which there shall neither be earing nor harvest."

"And God sent me before you to preserve you a posterity in the earth, and to save your lives by a great deliverance."

"So now it was not you that sent me hither, but God: and he hath made me a father to Pharaoh, and lord of all his house, and a ruler throughout all the land of Egypt."

My proposal is...Joseph's eagerness to use his blessings (gifts) to enable the Egyptians to get ready for a long time of starvation (famine) likewise permitted God's plans to be fulfilled.

(Genesis 45:4-8)

"Howbeit we speak wisdom among them that are perfect: yet not the wisdom of this world, nor of the princes of this world, that come to nought:"

"But we speak the wisdom of God in a mystery, even the hidden wisdom, which God ordained before the world unto our glory:"

"Which none of the princes of this world knew: for had they known it, they would not have crucified the Lord of glory."

The wisdom we speak of is the mystery (secret) wisdom of God, which was hidden in former times, but he made it for our benefit before the world began (before the foundation of the world, before Creation).

God's plan of redemption was established even before Creation itself.

(I Corinthians 2:6-8)

"If ye have heard of the dispensation of the grace of God which is given me to you-ward:"

"How that by revelation he made known unto me the mystery; (as I wrote afore in few words,"

"Whereby, when ye read, ye may understand my knowledge in the mystery of Christ)"

"Which in other ages was not made known unto the sons of men, as it is now revealed unto his holy apostles and prophets by the Spirit;"

"That the Gentiles should be fellowheirs, and of the same body, and partakers of his promise in Christ by the gospel:"

"Whereof I was made a minister, according to the gift of the grace of God given unto me by the effectual working of his power."

And this is the secret plan: The Gentiles have an equal share with the Jews in all the riches inherited by God's children.

God's plan to save mankind incorporated a plan for both Jew and Gentile.

(Ephesians 3:2-7)

32. If God has a plan, why should I even try to plan?

"This is the thing which I have spoken unto Pharaoh: What God is about to do sheweth unto Pharaoh."

"Behold, thyere come seven years of great plenty throughout all the land of Egypt:"

"And there shall arise after them seven years of famine; and all the plenty shall be forgotten in the land of Egypt; and famine shall consume the land;"

"And the plenty shall not be known in the land by reason of that famine following; for it shall be very grievous."

"And for that the dream was doubled unto Pharaoh twice; it is because the thing is established by God, and God will shortly bring it to pass."

"Now therefore let Pharaoh look out a man discreet and wise, and set him over the land of Egypt."

"Let Pharaoh do this, and let him appoint officers over the land, and take up the fifth part of the land of Egypt in the seven plenteous years."

"And let them gather all the food of those good years that come, and lay up corn under the hand of Pharaoh, and let them keep food in the cities."

"And that food shall be for store to the land against the seven years of famine, which shall be in the land of Egypt; that the land perish not through the famine."

Joseph's readiness and willingness to use his gifts to enable the Egyptians to get ready for a long time of famine also allowed God's plan to be fulfilled.

(Genesis 41:28-36)

"So I came to Jerusalem, and was there three days."

"And I arose in the night, I and some few men with me; neither told I any man what my God had put in my heart to do at Jerusalem: neither was there any beast with me, save the beast that I rode upon."

"And I went out by night by the gate of the valley, even before the dragon well, and to the dung port, and viewed the walls of Jerusalem, which were broken down, and the gates thereof were consumed with fire."

"Then I went on to the gate of the fountain, and to the king's pool: but there was no place for the beast that was under me to pass."

"Then went I up in the night by the brook, and viewed the wall, and turned back, and entered by the gate of the valley, and so returned."

"And the rulers knew not whither I went, or what I did; neither had I as yet told it to the Jews, nor to the priests, nor to the nobles, nor to the rulers, nor to the rest that did the work."

"Then said I unto them, Ye see the distress that we are in, how Jerusalem lieth waste, and the gates thereof are burned with fire; come, and let us build up the wall of Jerusalem, that we be no more a reproach."

Nehemiah exhibited wise and keen authority when he painstakingly arranged his undertaking before beginning to rebuild the wall of Jerusalem.

(Nehemiah 2:11-17)

"Go to now, ye that say, To day or to morrow we will go into such a city, and continue there a year, and buy and sell, and get gain:"

"Whereas ye know not what shall be on the morrow. For what is your life? It is even a vapour, that appeareth for a little time, and then vanisheth away."

"For that ye ought to say, If the Lord will, we shall live, and do this or that."

"But now ye rejoice in your boastings: all such rejoicing is evil."

What you should say is, "If the Lord wants us to, we will live and do this or that"...

All our planning is useless without God.

(James 4:13-16)

PROMISE FROM GOD

"There are many devices in a man's heart; nevertheless the counsel of the LORD, that shall stand."

You can make many plans, but the Lord's purpose will prevail.

(Proverbs 19:21)

POOR

33. Doesn't God care that I'm poor? I feel so lonely when I realize how so many others seem to have all they need and I'm struggling.

"For thou hast been a strength to the poor, a strength to the needy in his distress, a refuge from the storm, a shadow from the heat, when the blast of the terrible ones is as a storm against the wall."

(Isaiah 25:4)

"Let your conversation be without covetousness; and be content with such things as ye have: for he hath said, I WILL NEVER LEAVE THEE, NOR FORSAKE THEE."

(Hebrews 13:5)

"Who shall separate us from the love of Christ? Shall tribulation, or distress, or persecution, or famine, or nakedness, or peril, or sword?"

"As it is written, FOR THY SAKE WE ARE KILLED ALL THE DAY LONG; WE ARE ACCOUNTED AS SHEEP FOR THE SLAUGHTER."

"Nay, in all these things we are more than conquerors through him that loved us."

(Romans 8:35-37)

34. Does God really care about the poor?

"All my bones shall say, LORD, who is like unto thee, which deliverest the poor from him that is too strong for him, yea, the poor and the needy from him that spoileth him?"

Who else rescues the weak and helpless from the strong? Who else protects the poor and needy from those who want to rob them?

(Psalm 35:10)

"But I am poor and needy; yet the Lord thinketh upon me: thou art my help and my deliverer; make no tarrying, O my God."

I am poor and needy, but the Lord is thinking about me right now...

(Psalm 40:17)

"For he shall deliver the needy when he crieth; the poor also, and him that hath no helper."

(Psalm 72:12)

"He will regard the prayer of the destitute, and not despise their prayer."

(Psalm 102:17)

"Who humbleth himself to behold the things that are in heaven, and in the earth!"

"He raiseth up the poor out of the dust, and lifeth the needy out of the dunghill;"

"That he may set him with princes, even with the princes of his people."

God cares deeply for the poor and the needy. And he commands all believers to care for them, too.

(Psalm 113:6-8)

35. What is my responsibility to the poor?

"And if thy brother that dwelleth by thee be waxen poor, and be sold unto thee; thou shalt not compel him to serve as a bondservant:"

(Leviticus 25:39)

"He that hath pity upon the poor lendeth unto the LORD; and that which he hath given will he pay him again."

I you help the poor, you are lending to the LORD- and he will repay you!

(Proverbs 19:17)

"He that hath a bountiful eye shall be blessed; for he giveth of his bread to the poor."

(Proverbs 22:9)

"And if thou draw out thy soul to the hungry, and satisfy the afflicted soul; then shall thy light rise in obscurity, and thy darkness be as the noon day:"

Feed the hungry and help those in a tough situation. At that point your light will shine out from the darkness, and the darkness around you will be as brilliant as day.

(Isaiah 58:10)

"Therefore all things whatsoever ye would that men should do to you, do ye even so to them: for this is the law and the prophets."

Do for others what you would like them to do for you.

(Matthew 7:12)

"My brethren, have not the faith of our Lord Jesus Christ, the Lord of glory, with respect of persons."

"For if there come unto your assembly a man with a gold ring, in goodly apparel, and there come in also a poor man in vile raiment;"

"And ye have respect to him that weareth the gay clothing, and say unto him, Sit thou here in a good place; and say to the poor, Stand thou there, or sit here under my footstool:"

"Are ye not then partial in yourselves, and are become judges of evil thoughts?"

"Hearken, my beloved brethren, Hath not God chosen the poor of this world rich in faith, and heirs of the kingdom which he hath promised to them that love him?"

"But ye have despised the poor. Do not rich men oppress you, and draw you before the judgment seats?"

"Do not they blaspheme that worthy name by which ye are called?"

"If ye fulfil the royal law according to the scripture, THOU SHALT LOVE THY NEIGHBOUR AS THYSELF, ye do well:"

"But if ye have respect to persons, ye commit sin, and are convinced of the law as transgressors."

God has compassion for poor people, so in the event that we would be faithful, we should have compassion for poor people. Compassion that doesn't venture into our checkbooks or onto our schedule is philosophical passion, not godly passion. Helping the poor isn't only a commitment but a privilege that ought to bring us great joy.

(James 2:1-9)

PROMISE FROM GOD

"For ye know the grace of our Lord Jesus Christ, that, though he was rich, yet for your sakes he became poor, that ye through his poverty might be rich."

You know how full of with love and kindness our Lord Jesus Christ was. Despite the fact that he was rich, yet for the well-being of you he became very poor, so that by the neediness (poverty) he could make you rich.

(II Corinthians 8:9)

PRAISE

36. How are we to express our praise to God?

"Praise ye the LORD. Sing unto the LORD a new song, and his praise in the congregation of saints."

"Let Israel rejoice in him that made him: let the children of Zion be joyful in their King."

"Let them praise his name in the dance: let them sing praises unto him with the timbrel and harp."

"For the LORD taketh pleasure in his people: he will beautify the meek with salvation."

"Let the saints be joyful in glory: let them sing aloud upon their beds."

"Let the high praises of God be in their mouth, and a twoedged sword in their hand."

"To execute vengeance upon the heathen, and punishments upon the people;"

"To bind their kings with clains, and their nobles with fetters of iron;"

"To execute upon them the judgment written: this honour have all his saints. Praise ye the LORD."

"Praise ye the LORD. Praise God in his sanctuary: praise him in the firmament of his power."

"Praise him for his mighty acts: praise him according to his excellent greatness."

"Praise him with the sound of the trumpet: praise him with the psaltery and harp."

"Praise him with the timbrel and dance: praise with stringed instruments and organs."

"Praise him upon the loud cymbals: praise him upon the high sounding cymbals."

"Let every thing that hath breath praise the LORD. Praise ye the LORD."

Let everything that lives sing praises to the LORD!

The people of God are exhorted to praise him with singing, music, and great joy."

(Psalm 149:1-9, 150:1-6)

"By him therefore let us offer the sacrifice of praise to God continually, that is, the fruit of our lips giving thanks to his name."

When we tell others of Christ's name we are offering him a sacrifice of praise.

(Hebrews 13:15)

"I hate, I despise your feast days, and I will not smell in your solemn assemblies."

"Though ye offer me burnt offerings and your meat offerings, I will not accept them:

neither will I regard the peace offerings of your fat beasts."

"Take thou away from me the noise of thy songs; for I will not hear the melody of thy viols."

"But let judgment run down as waters, and righteousness as a mighty stream."

Our praise must be sincere and not hypocritical.

(Amos 5:21-24)

37. Why do we praise God?

"To the praise of the glory of his grace, wherein he hath made us accepted in the beloved."

"In whom we have redemption through his blood, the forgiveness of sins, according to the riches of his grace;"

"Wherein he hath abounded toward us in all wisdom and prudence;"

"Having made known unto us the mystery of his will, according to his good pleasure which he hath purposed in himself:"

"That in the dispensation of the fulness of times he might gather together in one all things in Christ, both which are in heaven, and which are on earth; even in him:"

"In whom also we have obtained an inheritance, being predestinated according to the purpose of him who worketh all things after the counsel of his own will."

"That we should be to the praise of his glory, who first trusted in Christ."

For providing his gracious salvation God deserves our praise.

(Ephesians 1:6-12)

"Bless the LORD, O my soul: and all that is within me, bless his holy name."

"Bless the LORD, O my soul, and forget not all his benefits:"

"Who forgiveth all thine iniquities; who healeth all thy diseases;"

"Who redeemethy thy life from destruction; who crowneth thee with lovingkindness and tender mercies;"

"Who satisfieth thy mouth with good things; so that thy youth is renewed like the eagle's."

"The LORD executeth righteousness and judgment for all that are oppressed."

"He made known his ways unto Moses, his acts unto the children of Israel."

"The LORD is merciful and gracious, slow to anger, and plenteous in mercy."

"He will not always chide; neither will he keep his anger for ever."

"He hath not dealt with us after our sins; nor rewarded us according to our iniquities."

"For as the heaven is high above the earth, so great is his mercy toward them that fear him."

"As far as the east is from the west, so far hath he removed our transgressions from us."

"Like as a father pitieth his children, so the LORD pitieth them that fear him."

"For he knoweth our frame; he remembereth that we are dust."

"As for man, his days are as grass: as a flower of the field, so he flourisheth."

"For the wind passeth over it, and it is gone; and the place thereof shall know it no more."

"But the mercy of the LORD is from everlasting to everlasting upon them that fear him, and his righteousness unto children's children;"

"To such as keep his covenant, and to those that remember his commandments to do them."

"The LORD hath prepared his throne in the heavens; and his kingdom ruleth over all."

"Bless the LORD, ye his angels, that excel in strength, that do his commandments, hearkening unto the voice of his word."

"Bless ye the LORD, all ye his hosts; ye ministers of his, that do his pleasure."

"Bless the LORD, all his works in all places of his dominion: bless the LORD, O my soul."

We praise God for his forgiveness, healing, and salvation.

(Psalm 103:1-22)

"I WILL extol thee, my God, O king; and I will bless thy name for ever and ever."

"Every day will I bless thee; and I will praise thy name for ever and ever."

"Great is the LORD, and greatly to be praised; and his greatness is unsearchable."

"One generation shall praise thy works to another, and shall declare thy mighty acts."

"I will speak of the glorious honour of thy majesty, and of thy wondrous works."

"And men shall speak of the might of thy terrible acts: and I will declare thy greatness."

"They shall abundantly utter the memory of thy great goodness, and shall sing of thy righteousness."

"The LORD is gracious, and full of compassion; slow to anger, and of great mercy."

"The LORD is good to all: and his tender mercies are over all his works."

"All thy works shall praise thee, O LORD; and thy saints shall bless thee."

"They shall speak of the glory of thy kingdom, and talk of thy power;"

"To make known to the sons of men his mighty acts; and the glorious majesty of his kingdom."

"Thy kingdom is an everlasting kingdom, and thy dominion endureth throughout all generations."

"The LORD upholdeth all that fall, and raiseth up all those that be bowed down."

"The eyes of all wait upon thee; and thou givest them their meat in due season."

"Thou openest thine hand, and satisfied the desire of every living thing."

"The LORD is righteous in all his ways, and holy in all his works."

"The LORD is nigh unto all them that call upon him, to all that call upon him in truth."

"He will fulfill the desire of them that fear him: he also will hear their cry, and will save them."

"The LORD preserveth all them that love him: but all the wicked will he destroy."

"My mouth shall speak the praise of the LORD: and let all flesh bless his holy name for ever and ever."

"Praise ye the LORD. Praise the LORD, O my soul."

"While I live will I praise the LORD: I will sing praises unto my God while I have any being."

"Put not your trust in princes, nor in the son of man, in whom there is no help."

"His breath goeth forth, he returneth to his earth; in that very day his thoughts perish."

"Happy is he that hath the God of Jacob for his help, whose hope is in the LORD his God."

"Which made heaven, and earth, the sea, and all that therein is: which keepeth truth for ever:"

"Which executeth judgment for the oppressed: which giveth food to the hungry. The LORD looseth the prisoners:"

"The LORD openeth the eyes of the blind: the LORD raiseth them that are bowed down:

the LORD loveth the righteous:"

"The LORD preserveth the strangers; he relieveth the fatherless and widow: but the way of the wicked he turneth upside down."

"The LORD shall reign for ever, even thy God, O Zion, unto all generations.

Praise ye the LORD."

We praise God for his eterenal and unchanging qualities.

(Psalm 145:1-21; 146:1-10)

"And as he went, they spread their clothes in the way."

"And when he was come nigh, even now at the descent of the mount of Olives, the whole multitude of the disciples began to rejoice and praise God with a loud voice for all the mighty works that they had seen;"

'Saying, BLESSED BE THE KING THAT COMETH IN THE NAME OF THE LORD:

peace in heaven, and glory in the highest."

"And some of the Pharisees from among the multitude said unto him, Master, rebuke thy disciples."

"And he answered and said unto them, I tell you that, if these should hold their peace, the stones would immediately cry out."

If they stayed quiet, the stones along the road would cry out.

If we don't lift our voices in praise of Jesus as our Lord and King, the very rocks and stones will shout out!

(Luke 19:36-40)

PROMISE FROM GOD

"When he shall come to be glorified in his saints, and to be admired in all them that believe (because our testimony among you was believed) in that day."

(II Thessalonians 1:10)

PRAYER

38. What is prayer?

"If my people, which are called by my name, shall humble themselves, and pray, and seek my face, and turn from their wicked ways; then will I hear from heaven, and will forgive their sin, and will heal their land."

Prayer is an act of humble worship in which we seek God with all our heart.

(II Chronicles 7:14)

"For in thee, O LORD, do I hope: thou wilt hear, O LORD my God."

"For I said, Hear me, lest otherwise they should rejoice over me: when my foot slippeth, they magnify themselves against me."

But I confess my sins; I am deeply sorry for what I have done.

(Psalm 38:15, 16)

"If we confess our sins, he is faithful and just to forgive us our sins, and to cleanse us from all unrighteousness."

Prayer often begins with a confession of sin.

(I John 1:9)

"And Saul said, Let us go down after the Phi-lis'-tines by night, and spoil them until the morning light, and let us not leave a man of them. And they said, Do whatsoever seemeth good unto thee. Then said the priest, Let us draw near hither unto God."

"And Saul asked counsel of God, Shall I go down after the Phi-lis'-tines? Wilt thou deliver them into the hand of Israel? But he answered him not that day."

"And Saul said, Draw ye near hither, all the chief of the people; and know and see wherein this sin hath been this day."

"For, as the LORD liveth, which saveth Israel, though it be in Jonathan my son, he shall surely die. But there was not a man among all the people that answered him."

"Then said he unto all Israel, Be ye on one side, and I and Jonathan my son will be on the other side. And the people said unto Saul, Do what seemeth good unto thee."

"Therefore Saul said unto the LORD God of Israel, Give a perfect lot. And Saul and Jonathan were taken: but the people escaped."

"And Saul said, Cast lots between me and Jonathan my son. And Jonathan was taken."

"Then Saul said to Jonathan, tell me what thou hast done. And Jonathan told him, and said, I did but taste a little honey with the end of the rod that was in mine hand, and, lo, I must die."

"And Saul answered, God do so and more also: for thou shalt surely die, Jonathan."

"And the people said unto Saul, Shall Jonathan die, who hath wrought this great salvation in Israel? God forbid: as the LORD liveth, there shall not one hair of his head fall to the ground; for he hath wrought with God this day. So the people rescued Jonathan, that he died not."

Prayer is asking God first.

(I Samuel 14:36-45)

"But when the Phi-lis'-tines heard that they had anointed David king over Israel, all the Phi-lis'-tines cam up to seek David; and David heard of it, and went down to the hold."

"The Phi-lis'-tines also came and spread themselves in the valley of Reph'-a-im."

"And David enquired of the LORD, saying, Shall I go up to the Phi-lis'-tines? wilt thou deliver them into mine hand? And the LORD said unto David, Go up; for I will doubtless deliver the Phi-lis'-tines into thine hand."

Prayer is asking God for guidance and waiting for his direction and leading.

(II Samuel 5:17-19)

"And in the morning, rising up a great while before day, he went out, and departed into a solitary place, and there prayed."

Prayer is an expression of an intimate relationship with our heavenly Father, who makes his own love and resources available to us.

(Mark 1:35)

"HE that dwelleth in the secret place of the most High shall abide under the shadow of the Almighty."

I will say of the LORD, He is my refuge and my fortress: my God, in him will I trust."

Through prayer we praise our mighty God, (And what a mighty God we serve)

(Psalm 9:1, 2)

39. Does the Bible teach a "right way" to pray?

"And it came to pass, when I heard these words, that I sat down and wept, and mourned certain days, and fasted, and prayed before the God of heaven."

"And said, I beseech thee, O LORD God of heaven, the great and terrible God, that keepeth covenant and mercy for them that love him and observe his commandments:"

"Let thine ear now be attentive, and thine eyes open, that thou mayest hear the prayer of thy servant, which I pray before thee now, day and night, for the children of Israel thy servants, and confess the sins of the children of Israel, which we have sinned against thee: both I and my father's house have sinned."

"We have dealt very corruptly against thee, and have not kept the commandments, nor the statutes, nor the judgments, which thou commandedst thy servant Moses."

"Remember, I beseech thee, the word that thou commandedst thy servant Moses, saying, If ye transgress, I will scatter you abroad among the nations:"

"But if ye turn unto me, and keep my commandments, and do them; though there were of you cast out unto the uttermost part of the heaven, yet will I gather them from thence, and will bring them unto the place that I have chosen to set my name there."

"Now these are thy servants and thy people, whom thou hast redeemed by thy great power, and by thy strong hand."

"O LORD, I beseech thee, let now thine ear be attentive to the prayer of thy servant, and to the prayer of thy servants, who desire to fear thy name: and prosper, I pray thee, thy servant this day, and grant him mercy in the sight of this man. For I was the king's cupbearer."

All through the Bible powerful prayer incorporates components of adoration, confession, and commitment, as well as requests.

(Nehemiah 1:4-11)

"And when thou prayest, thou shalt not be as the hypocrites are: for they love to pray standing in the synagogues and in the corners of the streets, that they may be seen of men. Verily I say unto you, They have their reward."

"But thou, when thou prayest, enter into thy closet, and when thou hast shut thy door, pray to thy Father which is in secret; and thy Father which seeth in secret shall reward thee openly."

"But when ye pray, use not vain repetitions, as the heathen do: for they think that they shall be heard for their much speaking."

"Be not ye therefore like unto them: for your Father knoweth what things ye have need of, before ye ask him."

"After this manner therefore pray ye: Our Father which art in heaven, Hallowed be thy name."

"Thy kingdom come. Thy will be done in earth, as it is in heaven."

"Give us this day our daily bread."

"And forgive us our debts, as we forgive our debtors."

"And lead us not into temptation, but deliver us from evil: For thine is the kingdom, and the power, and the glory, for ever.

A-men'."

Jesus showed his disciples that prayer is a personal relationship with the Father that incorporates a reliance for every day needs, commitment to obedience, and forgiveness of sin.

(Matthew 6:5-13)

"AND he spake a parable unto them to this end, that men ought always to pray, and not to faint;"

"Saying, There was in a city a judge, which feared not God, neither regarded man:"

"And there was a widow in that city; and she came unto him, saying, Avenge me of mine adversary."

"And he would not for a while: but afterward he said within himself, Though I fear not God, nor regard man;"

"Yet because this widow troubleth me, I will avenge her, lest by her continual coming she weary me."

"And the Lord said, Hear what the unjust judge saith."

"And shall not God avenge his own elect, which cry day and night unto him, though he bear long with them?"

"I tell you that he will avenge them speedily. Nevertheless when the Son of man cometh, shall he find faith on the earth?"

One day Jesus told his disciples a story to illustrate their need for constant prayer and to show them that they must never give up...

"Prayer is to be consistent and persistent."

(Luke 18:1-8)

"Then the king said unto me, For what dost thou make request? So I prayed to the God of heaven."

…...With a prayer to the God of heaven….

Prayer can be spontaneous.

(Nehemiah 2:4)

40. Does God always answer prayer?

"Is any among you afflicted? Let him pray. Is any merry/ let him sing psalms."

"Is any sick among you? Let him call for the elders of the church; and let them pray over him, anointing him with oil in the name of the Lord:"

"And the prayer of faith shall save the sick, and the Lord shall raise him up; and if he have committed sins, they shall be forgiven him."

"Confess your faults one to another, and pray one for another, that ye may be healed.

The effectual fervent prayer of a righteous man availeth much."

"E-li'-as was a man subject to like passions as we are, and he prayed earnestly that it might not rain: and it rained not on the earth by the space of three years and six months."

"And he prayed again, and the heaven gave rain, and the earth brought forth her fruit."

Confess your sins to each other and pray for each other so that you may be healed.

The earnest prayer of a righteous person has great power and wonderful results.

(James 5:13-18)

"And this is the confidence that we have in him, that, if we ask any thing according to his will, he heareth us:"

And if we know that he hear us, whatsoever we ask, we know that we have the petitions that we desired of him."

We can be confident of God's response to our prayer when we submit first to his will.

(I John 5:14, 15)

"And lest I should be exalted above measure through the abundance of the revelations, there was given to me a thorn in the flesh, the messenger of Satan to buffet me, lest I should be exalted above measure."

"For this thing I besought the Lord thrice, that it might depart from me."

"And he said unto me, My grace is sufficient for thee: for my strength is made perfect in weakness. Most gladly therefore will I rather glory in my infirmities, that the power of Christ may rest upon me."

"Therefore I take pleasure in infirmities, in reproaches, in necessities, in persecutions, in distresses for Christ's sake: for when I am weak, then am I strong."

In some cases, similar to Paul, we will find that God answers prayer by giving us not what we request but rather something better.

(II Corinthians 12:7-10)

"And the LORD said unto Moses, Wherefore criest thou unto me? Speak unto the children of Israel, that they go forward:"

Our prayer must be accompanied by a willingness to obey with our actions.

(Exodus 14:15)

PROMISE FROM GOD

"FOR THE EYES OF THE LORD ARE OVER THE RIGHTEOUS, AND HIS EARS ARE OPEN UNTO THEIR PRAYERS: BUT THE FACE OF THE LORD IS AGAINST THEM THAT DO EVIL."

(I Peter 3:12)

PREJUDICE

41. What does the Bible say about ethnic or racial prejudice?

"But a certain Sa-mar'-i-tan, as he journeyed, came where he was: and when he saw him, he had compassion on him."

Then a despised Samaritan came along, and when he saw the man, he felt deep pity.

(Luke 10:33)

""Then saith the woman of Sa-ma'-ri-a unto him, How is it that thou, being a Jew, askest drink of me, which am a woman of Sa-ma'-ria-a? For the Jews have no dealings with the Sa-mar'-i-tans."

(John 4:9)

"And he said unto them, Ye know how that it is an unlawful thing for a man that is a Jew to keep company, or come unto one of another nation; but God hath shewed me that I should not call any man common or unclean."

(Acts 10:28)

"Then Peter opened his mouth, and said, Of truth I perceive that God is no respecter of persons:"

"But in every nation he that feareth him, and worketh righteousness, is accepted with him."

(Acts 10:34, 35)

"When they heard these things, they held their peace, and glorified God, saying, Then hath God also to the Gentiles granted repentance unto life."

In heaven there are no ethnic gatherings, no races, no differentiations, for example, these, so for what reason would it be advisable for them to be significant at this point?

(Acts 11:18)

42. What are other areas the Bible warns us not to be prejudiced in?

APPEARANCE

"But the LORD said unto Samuel, Look not on his countenance, or on the height of his stature; because I have refused him: for the LORD seeth not as man seeth; for man looketh on the outward appearance, but the LORD looketh on the heart."

The LORD doesn't settle on choices the manner in which you do! People judge by outward appearance, but the LORD takes a look at a person's thoughts and intentions.

(I Samuel 16:7)

"For he shall grow up before him as a tender plant, and as a root out of a dry ground: he hath no form nor comeliness; and when we shall see him, there is a beauty that we should desire him."

Generalizations proliferate-bias against chubby (fat) individuals, short individuals, thin (skinny) individuals, ugly individuals, individuals with skin defects, bald individuals - the rundown continues forever. However, the genuine individual is inside; the body is just the shell, the brief lodging. It isn't right to pass judgment on an individual by the transitory house the person is in. The genuine individual inside might be an individual of mind boggling beauty.

(Isaiah 53:2)

ECONOMIC STATUS

"The poor is hated even of his own neighbour: but the rich hath many friends."

"He that despiseth his neighbour sinneth; but he that hath mercy on the poor, happy is he."

It is a sin to despise one's neighbours; blessed are those who help the poor.

(Proverbs 14:20, 21)

"He that oppresseth the poor reproacheth his Maker: but he that honoureth him hath mercy on the poor."

Those who oppress the poor insult their Master, but those who help the poor honor him."

(Proverbs 14:31)

"MY brethren, have not the faith of our Lord Jesus Christ, the Lord of glory, with respect of persons."

"For if there come unto your assembly a man with a gold ring, in goodly apparel, and there come in also a poor man in vile raiment;"

"And ye have respect to him that weareth the gay clothing, and say unto him, Sit thou here in a good place; and say to the poor, Stand thou there, or sit here under my footstool:"

"Are ye not then partial in yourselves, and are become judges of evil thoughts?"

"Hearken, my beloved brethren, Hath not god chosen the poor of this world rich in faith, and heirs of the kingdom which he hath promised to them that love him?"

"But ye have despised the poor. Do not rich men oppress you, and draw you before the judgment seats?"

"Do not they blaspheme that worthy name by the which ye are called?"

"If ye fulfill the royal law according to the scripture, THOU SHALT LOVE THY NEIGHBOUR AS THYSELF, ye do well:"

"But if ye have respect to persons, ye commit sin, and are convinced of the law as transgressors."

A rich individual and a poor individual come to church. Which is welcomed more? A well off individual and a poor individual shout out in a congregation board of trustees meeting. Which one do you tune in to most cautiously?

(James 2:1-9)

AGE

"Take heed that ye despise not one of these little ones; for I say unto you, That in heaven their angels do always behold the face of my Father which is in heaven."

How often have you heard the words "They're simply youngsters"? We don't have time for youngsters. We don't hear them out as much as we would to an adult. Actually, children are the genuine "celebrities" of the world, for in their grasp rests what's to come in the future.

(Matthew 18:10)

"Let no man despise thy youth; but be thou an example of the believers, in word, in conversation, in charity, in spirit, in faith, in purity."

Don't let anyone think little of you because you are young.

(I Timothy 4:12)

"REBUKE not an elder, but intreat him as a father; and the younger men as brethren;"

To youth belongs the future and to Old age belongs the honor of bringing us all to this point. Youth has the chance to win the world. Old age has the experience of victory.

We should honor each for its contributions and commitments.

(I Timothy 5:1)

OCCUPATION

"And when the sabbath day was come, he began to teach in the syngogue: and many hearing him were astonished, saying, From whence hath this man these things? And what wisdom is this which is given unto him, that even such mighty works are wrought by his hands?"

"Is not this the carpenter, the son of Mary, the brother of James, and Jo'-ses, and of Juda, and Simon? and are not his sisters here with us? And they were offended at him."

God doesn't discount families or occupations, and maybe that is the reason Jesus decided to go to the family of a woodworker (carpenter) as opposed to a family of a king. God loves each individual, paying little mind to occupation.

(Mark 6:2, 3)

43. Is the world prejudiced against Christ's followers?

"If ye were of the world, the world would love his own: but because ye are not of the world, but I have chosen you out of the world, therefore the world hateth you."

When an individual enjoys sin and wants to continue in it, it's normal to build up a hatred for Christ and his followers.

(John 15:19)

PROMISE FROM GOD

"And above all these things put on charity, which is the bond of perfectness."

And the most important piece of clothing you must wear is love.

Love is what binds us all together in perfect harmony.

(Colossians 3:14)

PRESENCE OF GOD

44. How can I experience God's presence in my life?

"If my people, which are called by my name, shall humble themselves, and pray, and seek my face, and turn from their wicked ways; then will I hear from heaven, and will forgive their sin, and will heal their land."

God reveals himself when we seek him and turn away from sin.

(II Chronicles 7:14)

"One thing have I desired of the LORD, that will I seek after; that I may dwell in the house of the LORD all the days of my life, to behold the beauty of the LORD, and to enquire in his temple."

We can know God through earnest and sincere worship.

(Psalm 27:4)

"For I know the thoughts that I think toward you, saith the LORD, thoughts of peace, and not of evil, to give you an expected end."

"Then shall ye call upon me, and ye shall go and pray unto me, and I will hearken unto you."

"And ye shall seek me, and find me, when ye shall search for me with all your heart."

Seeking and finding God requires consistent and purposeful prayer.

(Jeremiah 29:11-13)

"Ask, and it shall be given you; seek, and ye shall find; knock, and it shall be opened unto you:"

"For every one that asketh receiveth; and he that seeketh findeth; and to him that knocketh it shall be opened."

"Or what man is there of you, whom if his son ask bread, will he give him a stone?"

"Or if he ask a fish, will he give him a serpent?"

"If ye then, being evil, know how to give good gifts unto your children, how much more shall your Father which is in heaven give good things to them that ask him?"

God welcomes us to move toward him as a child moves toward a caring and loving father.

(Matthew 7:7-11)

45. What do I do when it feels like God is far away?

"O LORD, thou hast searched me, and known me."

"Thou knowest my downsitting and mine uprising, thou understandest my thought afar off."

"Thou compassest my path and my lying down, and art acquainted with all my ways."

"For there is not a word in my tongue, but, lo, O LORD, thou knowest it altogether."

"Thou hast beset me behind and before, and laid thine hand upon me."

"Such knowledge is too wonderful for me; it is high, I cannot attain unto it."

"Whither shall I go from thy spirit? Or whither shall I flee from thy presence?"

"If I ascend up into heaven, thou art there: if I make my bed in hell, behold, thou art there."

"If I take the wings of the morning, and dwell in the uttermost parts of the sea;"

"Even there shall thy hand lead me, and thy right hand shall hold me."

"If I say, Surely the darkness shall cover me; even the night shall be light about me."

"Yea, the darkness hideth not from thee; but the night shineth as the day: the darkness and the light are both alike to thee."

I can never escape from your spirit! I can never escape from your presence!

There is no height nor depth to which God won't go to be with us.

(Psalm 139:1-12)

"Behold, I go forward, but he is not there; and backward, but I cannot perceive him:"

Faith is trusting God even when we feel far from Him.

(Job 23:8)

46. Does the Lord want to be with us and will he respond when we seek him?

"But if from thence thou shalt seek the LORD thy God, thou shalt find him, if thou seek him with all thy heart and with all thy soul."

(Deuteronomy 4:29)

"Have not I commanded thee? Be strong and of good courage; be not afraid, neither be thou dismayed: for the LORD thy God is with thee whithersoever thou goest."

(Joshua 1:9)

"Draw nigh to God, and he will draw nigh to you. Cleanse you hands, ye sinners; and purify your hearts, ye double minded."

Draw close to God, and he will draw close to you.

(James 4:8)

"Behold, I stand at the door, and knock: If any man hear my voice, and open the door, I will come in to him, and will sup with him, and he with me."

(Revelation 3:20)

Dr. John Thomas Wylie

47. How did Christ's sacrificial death make it possible for us to live in the presence of the Lord?

"By a new and living way, which he hath consecrated for us, through the veil, that is to say, his flesh:"

When we live in concordance with the Lord, it is joy and delight to wait in his presence.

(Hebrews 10:20)

"Thou wilt shew me the path of life: in thy presence is fulness of joy; at thy right hand there are pleasures for evermore."

(Psalm 16:11)

"Lord, I have loved the habitation of thy house, and the place where thine honour dwelleth."

(Psalm 26:8)

"For thou hast made him most blessed for ever: thou hast made him exceeding glad with thy countenance."

You have endowed him with eternal blessings. You have given him the joy of being in your presence.

(Psalm 21:6)

"Thou shalt hide them in the secret of thy presence from the pride of man; thou shalt keep them secretly in a pavilion from the strife of tongues."

(Psalm 31:20)

"Sing unto God, sing praises to his name: extol him that rideth upon the heavens by his name JAH, and rejoice before him."

(Psalm 68:4)

"He will not suffer thy foot to be moved: he that keepeth thee will not slumber."

"Behold, he that keepeth Israel shall neither slumber nor sleep."

(Psalm 121:3, 4)

48. When are we afraid of the presence of the Lord?

"And they heard the voice of the LORD God walking in the garden in the cool of the day: and Adam and his wife hid themselves from the presence of the LORD God amongst the trees of the garden."

The presence of sin in our lives makes us dread the presence of the Lord, for he will most likely find us out.

(Genesis 3:8)

"Hold thy peace at the presence of the LORD GOD: for the day of the LORD is at hand:

for the LORD hath prepared a sacrifice, he hath bid his guests."

To walk in God's presence with a heart bent toward sin is to invite the Lord's judgement.

(Zephaniah 1:7)

PROMISE FROM GOD

"But if we walk in the light, as he is in the light, we have fellowship one with another, and the blood of Jesus Christ his Son cleanseth us from all sin."

(I John 1:7)

PRIDE

49. Why is pride considered one of the "seven deadly sins" when other things seem so much worse?

"Moreover the word of the LORD came unto me, saying,"

"Son of man, take up a lamentation upon the king of Ty'-rus, and say unto him, This saith the LORD GOD; Thou sealest up the sum, full of wisdom, and perfect in beauty."

"Thou hast been in Eden the garden of God; every precious stone was thy covering, the sardius, topaz, and the diamond, the beryl, the onyx, and the jasper, the sapphire, the emerald, and the carbuncle, and gold: the workmanship of thy tabrets and of thy pipes was prepared in thee in the day that thou wast created."

"Thou art the anointed cherub that covereth; and I have set thee so: thou wast upon the holy mountain of God; thou hast walked up and down in the midst of the stone of fire."

"Thou wast perfect in thy ways from the day that thou wast created, till iniquity was found in thee."

By the multitude of thy merchandise they have filled the midst of thee with violence, and thou hast sinned: therefore I will cast thee as profane out of the mountain of God:

and I will destroy thee, O covering cherub, from the midst of the stones of fire."

"Thine heart was lifted up because of thy beauty, thou hast corrupted thy wisdom by reason of thy brightness: I will cast thee to the ground, I will lay thee before kings, that they may behold thee."

"Thou hast defiled thy sanctuaries by the multitude of thine iniquities, by the iniquity of thy traffick; therefore will I bring forth a fire from the midst of thee, it shall devour thee, and I will bring thee to ashes upon the earth in the sight of all them that behold thee."

"All they that know thee among the people shall be astonished at thee: thou shalt be a terror, and never shalt thou be any more."

The Bible appears to show that pride was the sin that brought about Lucifer (Satan) being cast from heaven.

(Ezekiel 28:11-19)

"The wicked in his pride doth persecute the poor: let them be taken in the devices that they have imagined."

"For the wicked boasteth of his heart's desire, and blesseth the covetous, whom the Lord abhorreth."

"The wicked, through the pride of his countenance, will not seek after God: God is not in all his thoughts."

"His ways are always grievous; thy judgments are far above out of his sight: as for all his enemies, he puffeth at them."

"He hath said in his heart, I shall not be moved: for I shall never be in adversity."

"His mouth is full of cursing and deceit and fraud: under his tongue is mischief and vanity."

"He sitteth in the lurking places of the villages: in the secret places doth he murder the innocent: his eyes are privily set against the poor."

"He lieth in wait secretly as a lion in his den: he lieth in wait to catch the poor: he doth catch the poor, when he draweth him into his net."

"He croucheth, and humbleth himself, that the poor may fall by his strong ones."

Pride leads to ignoring God and a life of disobedience.

(Psalm 10:2-11)

"For men shall be lovers of their own selves, covetous, boasters, proud, blasphemers, disobedient to parents, unthankful, unholy."

"Without natural affection, trucebreakers, false accusers, incontinent, fierce, despisers of those that are good."

"Traitors, heady, highminded, lovers of pleasures more than lovers of God;"

"Having a form of godliness, but denying the power thereof: from such turn away."

"For of this sort are they which creep into houses, and lead captive silly women laden with sins, led away with diver lusts,"

"Ever learning, and never able to come to the knowledge of the truth."

"Now as Jan'-nes and Jam'-bres withstood Moses, so do these also resist the truth: men of corrupt minds, reprobate concerning the faith."

"But they shall proceed no further; for their folly shall be manifest unto all men, as their's also was."

"But thou hast fully known my doctrine, manner of life, purpose, faith, longsuffering, charity, patience,"

Pride can demolish relationships quicker than nearly whatever else in light of the fact that it is continually detracting from others. Pride reinforces your position at the expense of others. Pride is childish, selfish.

(II Timothy 3:2-5)

"But when he was strong, his heart was lifted up to his destruction: for he transgressed against the LORD his God, and went into the temple of the LORD to burn incense upon the altar of incense.

"And Az'-a-ri'-ah the priest went in after him, and with him fourscore priests of the LORD, that were valiant men:"

"And they withstood Uz-zi'-ah the king, and said unto him, It appertaineth not unto thee, Uz-ai'-ah, to burn incense unto the LORD, but to the priests the sons of Aaron, that are consecrated to burn incense: go out of the sanctuary; for thou hast trespassed; neither shall it be for thine honour from the LORD God."

'Then Uz-zi'-ah was wroth, and had a censer in his hand to burn incense: and while he was wroth with the priests, the leprosy even rose up in his forehead before the priest in the house of the LORD, from beside the incense altar."

"And Az-a-ri'-ah the chief priest, and all the priests, looked upon him, and, behold, he was leprous in his forehead, and they thrust him out from thence; yea, himself hasted also to go out, because the LORD had smitten him."

A swelled estimation of our past victories prompts prideful conduct and, eventually, judgment.

(II Chronicles 26:16-20)

"The pride of thine heart hath deceived thee, thou that dwellest in the clefts of the rock, whose habitation is high; that saith in his heart, Who shall bring me down to the ground?"

Pride finds comfort in false security.

(Obadiah 1:3)

"And these things, brethren, I have in a figure transferred to myself and to A-pol'-los for your sakes; that ye might learn in us not to think of men above that which is written, that no one of you be puffed up for one against another."

"For who maketh thee to differ from another? and what hast thou that thou didst not receive? Now if thou didst receive it, why dost thou glory, as if thou hadst not received it?"

Pride can taint our spiritual lives and divide the church.

(I Corinthians 4:6-7)

"And the people gave a shout, saying, It is the voice of a god, and not of a man."

"And immediately the angel of the Lord smote him, because he gave not God the glory:

and he was eaten of worms, and gave up the ghost."

God hates pride and will judge it severely.

(Acts 12:22, 23)

50. When is pride healthy and appropriate?

"I have therefore whereof I may glory through Jesus Christ in those things which pertain to God."

Paul was proud not of what he had achieved but of what God had done through him.

(Romans 15:17)

"Knowing therefore the terror of the Lord, we persuade men; but we are made manifest unto God; and I trust also are made manifest in your consciences."

"For we commend not ourselves again unto you, but give you occasion to glory on our behalf, that ye may have somewhat to answer them which glory in appearance, and not in heart."

"For whether we be beside ourselves, it is to God: or whether we be sober, it is for your cause."

Like Paul, if we take pride wholeheartedly in anything, we should have pride in the respectability (integrity) and genuineness (honesty) of our ministry and life.

(II Corinthians 5:11-13)

PROMISE FROM GOD

"Pride goeth before destruction, and an haughty spirit before a fall."

(Proverbs 16:18)

PRIORITIES

51. How do I know what's really important?

"Trust in the LORD with all thine heart; and lean not unto thine own understanding."

"In all thy ways acknowledge him, and he shall direct thy paths."

(Proverbs 3:5, 6)

"But many that are first shall be last; and the last first."

Putting God first is the most significant thing we can do. In the event that the entirety of your needs center around getting things done for yourself, they are misguided.

(Mark 10:31)

52. How do I set priorities?

"And if it seem evil unto you to serve the LORD, choose you this day whom ye will serve; whether the gods which your fathers served that were on the other side of the flood, or the gods of the Am'-or-ities, in whose land ye dwell: but as for me and my house, we will serve the LORD."

(Joshua 24:15)

"I have sent also unto you all my servants the prophets, rising up early and sending them, saying, Return ye now every man from his evil way, and amend your doings, and go not after other gods to serve them, and ye shall dwell in the land which I have given to you and to your fathers: but ye have not inclined your ear, nor hearkened unto me."

There is no more prominent need than loving and obeying God. Nothing influences (affects) our eternal future so remarkably.

(Jeremiah 35:15)

"Give therefore thy servant an understanding heart to judge thy people, that I may discern between good and bad: for who is able to judge this thy so great a people?"

Constantly seeking after God's wisdom is the best approach to discern right priorities.

(I Kings 3:9)

"And Saul said, Let us go down after the Phi-lis'-tines by night, and spoil them until the morning light, and let us not leave a man of the,. And they said, Do whatsoever seemeth good unto thee. Then said the priest, Let us draw near hither unto God."

We should speak with God first before setting priorities.

(I Samuel 14:36)

"But seek ye first the kingdom of God, and his righteousness; and all these things shall be added unto you."

Be deliberate about priorities. Set them and keep an eye on them first. At exactly that point will your life have its fullest importance.

(Matthew 6:33)

53. What happens when we fail to set priorities?

"In those days there was no king in Israel, but every man did that which was right in his own eyes."

When we fail to set priorities, we will stop doing what is right in God's eyes.

(Judges 17:6)

PROMISE FROM GOD

"Trust in the LORD with all thine heart; and lean not unto thine own understanding."

"In all thy ways acknowledge him, and he shall direct thy paths."

(Proverbs 3:5, 6)

PROCRASTINATION

54. Why do I procrastinate?
And is it really so bad?

"The slothful man saith, There is a lion in the way; a lion is in the streets."

The lazy person is full of excuses.

Making excuses is a favorite ploy of the procrastinator.

(Proverbs 26:13)

"NOW the word of the LORD came unto Jonah the son of A-mit'-tai, saying,"

"Arise, go to Nin'-e-veh, that great city, and cry against it; for their wickedness is come up before me."

"But Jonah rose up to flee unto Tar'-shish from the presence of the LORD, and went down to Jop'-pa; and he found a ship going to Tar'-shish: so he paid the fare thereof, and went down into it, to go with them unto Tar'-shish from the presence of the LORD."

Fear and rebellion made Jonah put off what he realized he ought to do.

(Jonah 1:1-3)

"AND the whole congregation of the children of Israel assembled together at Shi'-loh, and set up the tabernacle of the congregation there. And the land was subdued before them."

"And there remained among the children of Israel seven tribes, which had not yet received their inheritance."

"And Joshua said unto the children of Israel, How long are ye slack to go to possess the land, which the LORD God of your fathers hath given you?"

Procrastination is sometimes a form of disobedience.

(Joshua 18:1-3)

""For the kingdom of heaven is as a man travelling into a far country, who called his own servants, and delivered unto them his goods."

"And unto one he gave five talents, to another two, and to another one; to every man according to his several ability; and straightway took his journey."

"Then he that had received the five talents went and traded with the same, and made them other five talents."

"And likewise he that had received two, he also gained other two."

"But he that had received one went and digged in the earth, and hid his lord's money."

"After a long time the lord of those servants cometh, and reckoneth with them."

"And so he that had received five talents came and brought other five talents, saying, Lord, thou deliveredst unto me five talents; behold, I have gained beside them five talents more."

"His lord said unto him, Well done, thou good and faithful servant: thou hast been faithful over a few things, I will make thee ruler over many things: enter thou into the joy of thy lord."

"He also that had received two talents came and said, Lord, thou deliveredst unto me two talents: behold, I have gained two other talents beside them."

"His lord said unto him, Well done, good and faithful servant; thou hast been faithful over a few things, I will make thee ruler over many things: enter thou into the joy of thy lord."

"Then he which had received the one talent came and said, Lord, I knew that thou art an hard man, reaping where thou hast not sown, and gathering where thou hast not strawed:"

"And I was afraid, and went and hid thy talent in the earth: lo, there thou hast that is thine."

His lord answered and said unto him, Thou wicked and slothful servant, thou knewest that I reap where I sowed not, and gather where I have not strawed:"

"Thou oughtest therefore to have put my money to the exchangers, and then at my coming I should have received mine own with usury."

"Take therefore the talent from him, and give it unto him which hath ten talents."

"For unto every one that hath shall be given, and he shall have abundance: but from him that hath not shall be taken away even that which he hath."

"And cast ye the unprofitable servant into outer darkness: there shall be weeping and gnashing of teeth."

Fear of failure can lead to inaction and wasting our resources through procrastination.

(Matthew 25:14-30)

"Redeeming the time, because the days are evil,"

Make the most of every opportunity for doing good in these evil days.

Time is a blessing (a gift) from God and must not be wasted.

(Ephesians 5:16)

"THEN shall the kingdom of heaven be likened unto ten virgins, which took their lamps, and went forth to meet the bridegroom."

"And five of them were wise, and five were foolish."

"They that were foolish took their lamps, and took no oil with them:"

"But the wise took oil in their vessels with their lamps."

"While the bridegroom tarried, they all slumbered and slept."

"And at midnight there was a cry made, Behold, the bridegroom cometh; go ye out to meet him."

"Then all those virgins arose, and trimmed their lamps."

"And the foolish said unto the wise, Give us of your oil; for our lamps are gone out."

"But the wise answered, saying, Not so; lest there be not enough for us and you: but go ye rather to them that sell, and buy for yourselves."

"And while they went to buy, the bridegroom came; and they that were ready went in with him to the marriage: and the door was shut."

"Afterward came also the other virgins, saying, Lord, Lord, open to us."

"But he answered and said, Verily I say unto you, I know you not."

"Watch therefore, for ye know neither the day nor the hour wherein the Son of man cometh."

Inability to be prepared for the coming of Christ is the most costly form of spiritual procrastination.

(Matthew 25:1-13)

PROMISE FROM GOD

"Go to the ant, thou sluggard; consider her ways, and be wise:"

"Which having no guide, overseer, or ruler,"

"Provideth her meat in the summer, and gathereth her food in the harvest."

"How long wilt thou sleep, O sluggard? When wilt thou arise out of thy sleep?"

"Yet a little sleep, a little slumber, a little folding of the hands to sleep:"

"So shall thy poverty come as one that travelleth, and thy want as an armed man."

"A naughty person, a wicked man, walketh with a froward mouth."

"He winketh with his eyes, he speaketh with his feet, he teacheth with his fingers;"

Some additional rest, somewhat more sleep, a bit of collapsing of the hands to rest-and poverty will jump on you like a desperado...

(Proverbs 6:6-11)

Dr. John Thomas Wylie

PRODUCTIVITY

55. What does the Bible mean when it says our lives are to produce "good fruit"?

"BLESSED is the man that walketh not in the counsel of the ungodly, nor standeth in the way of sinners, nor sitteth in the seat of the scornful."

"But his delight is in the law of the LORD; and in his law doth he meditate day and night."

"And he shall be like a tree planted by the rivers of water, that bringeth forth his fruit in his season; his leaf also shall not wither; and whatsoever he doeth shall prosper."

(Psalm 1:1-3)

"NOW will I sing to my well-beloved a song of my beloved touching his vineyard. My well-beloved hath a vineyard in a very fruitful hill:"

"And he fenced it, and gathered out the stones thereof, and planted it with the choicest vine, and built a tower in the midst of it, and also made a winepress therein; and he looked that it should bring forth grapes, and it brought forth wild grapes."

"And now, O inhabitants of Jerusalem, and men of Judah, judge I pray you, betwixt me and my vineyard."

"What could have been done more to my vineyard, that I have not done in it?

Wherefore, when I looked that it should bring forth grapes, brought it forth wild grapes?"

"And now go to; I will tell you what I will do to my vineyard: I will take away the hedge thereof, and it shall be eaten up; and break down the wall thereof, and it shall be trodden down:"

"And I will lay it waste: it shall not be pruned, nor digged; but there shall come up briers and thorns: I will also command the clouds that they rain no rain upon it."

"For the vineyard of the LORD of hosts is the house of Israel, and the men of Judah has pleasant plant: and he looked for judgment, but behold oppression; for righteousness, but behold a cry."

God's people are to live lives that bear the product (fruit) of righteousness, equity (justice), and obedience to God's will.

(Isaiah 5:1-7)

"For a good tree bringeth not forth corrupt fruit; neither doth a corrupt tree bring forth\ good fruit."

"For every tree is known by his own fruit, For of thorns men do not gather figs, nor of a bramble bush gather they grapes."

"A good man out of the good treasure of this heart bringeth forth that which is good; and an evil man out of the evil treasure of his heart bringeth forth that which is evil; for of the abundance of the heart his mouth speaketh."

A tree is identified by the kind of fruit it produces...A good person produces good deeds from a good heart...

The fruit God wants is not the outside appearance of goodness through the trappings of religion, but the fruit of holy living.

(Luke 6:43-45)

56. How do we go about producing this "good fruit"?

"I AM the true vine, and my Father is the husbandman."

"Every branch in me that beareth not fruit he taketh away; and every branch that beareth fruit, he purgeth it, that it may bring forth more fruit."

"Now ye are clean through the word which I have spoken unto you."

"Abide in me, and I in you. As the branch cannot bear fruit of itself, except it abide in the vine; no more can ye, except ye abide in me."

"I am the vine, ye are the branches: He that abideth in me, and I in him, the same bringeth forth much fruit: for without me ye can do nothing."

"If a man abide not in me, he is cast forth as a branch, and is withered; and men gather them, and cast them into the fire, and they are burned."

"If ye abide in me, and my words abide in you, ye shall ask what ye will, and it shall be done unto you."

"Herein is my Father glorified, that ye bear much fruit; so shall ye be my disciples."

"As the Father hath loved me, so have I loved you: continue ye in my love."

Dr. John Thomas Wylie

"If ye keep my commandments, ye shall abide in my love; even as I have kept my Father's commandments, and abide in his love."

"These things have I spoken unto you, that my joy might remain in you, and that your joy might be full."

"This is my commandment, That ye love one another, as I have loved you."

"Greater love hath no man than this, that a man lay down his life for his friends."

"Ye are my friends, if ye do whatsoever I command you."

"Henceforth I call you not servants; for the servant knoweth not what his lord doeth; but I have called you friends; for all things that I have heard of my Father I have made known unto you."

Ye have not chosen me, but I have chosen you, and ordained you, that ye should go and briung forth fruit, and that your fruit should remain: that whatsoever ye shall ask of the Father in my name, he may give it you."

(John 15:1-16)

"This I say then, Walk in the Spirit, and ye shall not fulfill the lust of the flesh."

"For the flesh lusteth against the Spirit, and the Spirit against the flesh: and these are contrary the one to the other: so that ye cannot do the things that ye would."

"But if ye be led of the Spirit, ye are not under the law."

"Now the works of the flesh are manifest, which are these; Adultery, fornication, uncleanness, lasciviousness,"

"Idolatry, witchcraft, hatred, variance, emulations, wrath, strife, seditions, heresies,"

"Envying, murders, drunkenness, revellings, and such like: of the which I tell you before, as I have also told you in time past, that they which do such things shall not inherit the kingdom of God."

"But the fruit of the Spirit is love, joy, peace, longsuffering, gentleness, goodness, faith,"

"Meekness, temperance: against such there is no law."

"And they that are Christ's have crucified the flesh with the affections and lusts."

"If we live in the Spirit, let us also walk in the Spirit."

"Let us not be desirous of vain glory, provoking one another, envying one another."

But when the Holy Spirit controls our lives, he will produce this kind of fruit in us.

(Galatians 5:16-26)

"Wherefore, my brethren, ye also are become dead to the law by the body of Christ; that ye should be married to another; even to him who is raised from the dead, that we should bring forth fruit unto God."

"For when we were in the flesh, the motions of sins, which were by the law, did work in our members to bring forth fruit unto death."

"But now we are delivered from the law, that being dead wherein we were held; that we should serve in newness of spirit, and not in the oldness of the letter."

As a result of Jesus' power over death and the indwelling of his Holy Spirit, our old nature is killed, permitting our new nature to produce good fruit.

(Romans 7:4-6)

57. Should Christians care how productive they are at work or in business?

"He that tilleth his land shall be satisfied with bread; but he that followeth vain persons is void of understanding."

Hard work means prosperity; only fools idle away their time.

The Bible consistently teaches that hard work brings thriving (prosperity) and achievement (success).

(Proverbs 12:11)

"Now we command you, brethren, in the name of our Lord Jesus Christ, that ye withdraw yourselves from every brother that walketh disorderly, and not after the tradition which he received of us."

"For yourselves know how ye ought to follow us: for we behaved not ourselves disorderly among you;"

"Neither did we eat any man's bread for nought; but wrought with labour and travail night and day, that we might not be chargeable to any of you:"

"Not because we have not power, but to make ourselves an ensample unto you to follow us."

"For even when we were with you, this we commanded you, that if any would not work, neither should he eat."

Christians are relied upon to be beneficial so they don't become burdens to other people and bad examples to the world.

(II Thessalonians 5:6-10;)

PROMISE FROM GOD

"For unto every one that hath shall be given, and he shall have abundance: but from him that hath not shall be taken away even that which he hath."

(Matthew 25:29)

PROFANITY

58. "They're just words. Why is profanity such a big deal?

"Finally, brethren, whatsoever things are true, whatsoever things are honest, whatsoever things are just, whatsoever things are pure, whatsoever things are lovely, whatsoever things are of good report; if there be any virtue, and if there be any praise, think on these things."

"Those things, which ye have both learned, and received, and heard, and seen in me, do:

and the God of peace shall be with you."

Our minds are to be filled not with the profane but the holy.

(Philippians 4:8, 9)

"Thou shalt not take the name of the LORD thy God in vain; for the LORD will not hold him guiltless that taketh his name in vain."

Do not misuse the name of the LORD your God…

To use the name of God frivolously is to disregard God's standard for holiness.

(Exodus 20:7)

"And he that curseth his father, or his mother, shall surely be put to death."

To curse one's parents is as serious an offense as doing them physical mischief (harm).

(Exodus 21:17)

"Neither filthiness, nor foolish talking, nor jesting, which are not convenient: but rather giving of thanks."

Foul language has no part in a believer's vocabulary.

(Ephesians 5:4)

"In all things shewing thyself a pattern of good works: in doctrine shewing uncorruptiness, gravity, sincerity,"

"Sound speech, that cannot be condemned; that he that is of the contrary part may be ashamed, having no evil thing to say of you."

We are to take care that our speech is unadulterated and can't be condemned (criticized)

by the unbelieving world.

(Titus 2:7, 8)

PROMISE FROM GOD

"But I say unto you, That every idle word that men shall speak, they shall give account thereof in the day of judgment."

"For by thy words thou shalt be justified, and by thy words thou shalt be condemned."

(Matthew 12:36, 37)

PROMISES

59. With so little to depend upon in life, what can I count on from God?

"Is the law then against the promises of God? God forbid: for if there had been a law given which could have given life, verily righteousness should have been by the law."

"But the scripture hath concluded all under sin, that the promise by faith of Jesus Christ might be given to them that believe."

"But before faith came, we were kept under the law, shut up unto the faith which should afterwards be revealed."

"Wherefore the law was our schoolmaster to bring us unto Christ, that we might be justified by faith."

"But after that faith is come, we are no longer under a schoolmaster."

"For ye are all the children of God by faith in Christ Jesus."

"For as many of you as have been baptized into Christ have put on Christ."

"There is neither Jew nor Greek, there is neither bond nor free, there is neither male nor female: for ye are all one in Christ Jesus."

"And if ye be Christ's, then are ye Abraham's seed, and heirs according to the promise."

The center of God's promise has consistently been the offer of salvation through faith.

(Galatians 3:21-29)

"In whom ye also trusted, after that ye heard the word of truth, the gospel of your salvation: in whom also after that ye believed, ye were sealed with that holy Spirit of promise."

"Which is the earnest of our inheritance until the redemption of the purchased possession, unto the praise of his glory."

The Holy Spirit is God's guarantee that his promises are trustworthy.

(Ephesians 1:13, 14)

"Let not your heart be troubled; ye believe in God, believe also in me."

"In my Father's house are many mansions: if it were not so, I would have told you.

I go to prepare a place for you."

"And if I go and prepare a place for you, "I will come again, and receive you unto myself; that where I am, there ye may be also."

"And whither I go ye know, and the way ye know."

"Thomas saith unto him, Lord we know not whither thou goest; and how can we know the way?"

"Jesus saith unto him, I am the way, the truth, and the life: no man cometh unto the Father, but by me."

Jesus promises an eternal home in paradise for the those who trust him.

(John 14:1-6)

"If ye love me, keep my commandments."

"And I will pray the Father, and he shall give you another Comforter, that he may abide with you for ever;"

God is with us forever in the form of the Holy Spirit.

(John 14:15, 16)

"But, beloved, be not ignorant of this one thing, that one day is with the Lord as a thousand years, and a thousand years as one day."

"The Lord is not slack concerning his promise, as some men count slackness; but is longsuffering to usward, not willing that any should perish, but that all should come to repentance."

"But the day of the Lord will come as a thief in the night; in the which the heavens shall pass away with a great noise, and the elements shall melt with fervent heat, the earth also and the works that are therein shall be burned up."

The Bible promises that Jesus will come back to pass judgment on the world for its deeds.

(II Peter 3:8-10)

"And we know that all things work together for good to them that love God, to them who are the called according to his purpose."

God promises to redeem the events of our lives for our good if we look to him.

(Romans 8:28)

"That by two immutable things, in which it was impossible for God to lie, we might have a strong consolation, who have fled for refuge to lay hold upon the hope set before us:"

God's promises are totally trustworthy and dependable. This gives us extraordinary solace (comfort) in the present and assurance for what's to come in the future.

(Hebrews 6:18)

60. Why is it important to keep our promises?

"AND Moses spake unto the heads of the tribes concerning the children of Israel, saying, This is the thing which the LORD hath commanded."

"If a man vow a vow unto the LORD, or swear an oath to bind his soul with a bond; he shall not break his word, he shall do according to all that proceedeth out of his mouth."

Keeping a promise is the fundamental establishment for trust in any relationship.

(Numbers 30:1, 2)

"Again, ye have heard that it hath been said by them of old time, Thou shalt not forswear thyself, but shalt perform unto the Lord thine oaths:"

"But I say unto you, Swear not at all; neither by heaven; for it is God's throne:"

"Nor by the earth; for it is his footstool: neither by Jerusalem; for it is the city of the great King."

"Neither shalt thou swear by thy head, because thou canst not make one hair white or black."

"But let your communication be, Yea, yea; Nay, nay: for whatsoever is more than these cometh of evil."

Jesus said that if you are a person of your word, you shouldn't have to reinforce your promise with a vow. Staying faithful to your commitments promises) will establish your reputation as a person of your word.

(Matthew 5:33-37)

PROMISE FROM GOD

"Let us hold fast the profession of our faith without wavering; (for he is faithful that promised;)"

(Hebrews 10:23)

PROTECTION

61. Does God promise to protect us?

"Oh how great is thy goodness, which thou hast laid up for them that fear thee; which thou hast wrought for them that trust in thee before the sons of men!"

"Thou shalt hide them in the secret of thy presence from the pride of man: thou shalt keep them secretly in a pavilion from the strife of tongues."

"Blessed be the LORD; for he hath shewed me his marvellous kindness in a strong city."

"For I said in my haste, I am cut off from before thine eyes: nevertheless thou heardest the voice of my supplications when I cried unto thee."

"O love the LORD, all ye his saints: for the LORD preserveth the faithful, and plentifully rewardeth the proud doer."

"Be of good courage, and he shall strengthen your heart, all ye that hope in the LORD."

(Psalm 31:19-24)

"Sha'-drach, Me'-shach, and A-bed'-ne-go, answered and said to the king, O Neb-u-chad-nez'-zar, we are not careful to answer thee in this matter."

"If it be so, our God whom we serve is able to deliver us from the burning fiery furnace, and he will deliver us out of thine hand, O king."

"But if not, be it known unto thee, O king, that we will not serve thy gods, nor worship the golden image which thou hast set up."

God promises to protect and keep safe the individuals who love him. Be that as it may, a definitive fulfillment of this promise is in the spiritual protection of God's loving grace as opposed to physical protection. Like Daniel's companions, we should commit to obeying God regardless of what befalls our earthy body.

(Daniel 3:16-18)

"I have called upon thee, for thou wilt hear me, and hear my speech."

"Shew thy marvellous lovingkindness, O thou hast savest by thy right hand them which put their trust in thee from those that rise up against them."

"Keep me as the apple of the eye, hide me under the shadow of thy wings,"

"From the wicked that oppress me, from my deadly enemies, who compass me about."

"They are inclosed in their own fat: with their mouth they speak proudly."

"They have now compassed us in our steps: they have set their eyes bowing down to the earth;"

"Like as a lion that is greedy of his prey, and as it were a young lion lurking in secret places."

"Arise, O LORD, disappoint him, cast him down; deliver my soul from the wicked, which is thy sword:"

"From men which are thy hand, O LORD, from men of the world, which have their portion in this life, and whose belly thou fillest with thy hid treasure: they are full of children, and leave the rest of their substance to their babes."

"As for me, I will behold thy face in righteousness; I shall be satisfied, when I awake, with thy likeness."

The psalmist prays to God for protection from foes but believes that extreme well-being (Ultimate safety) is God's salvation that leads to the hope of heaven.

(Psalm 17:6-15)

"Be careful for nothing; but in every thing by prayer and supplication with thanksgiving let your requests be made known unto God."

"And the peace of God, which passeth all understanding, shall keep your hearts and minds through Christ Jesus."

Through consistent and devoted prayer we can know the protection of God's supernatural peace.

(Philippians 4:6, 7)

"THEN all the captains of the forces, and Jo-ha'-nan the son of Ka-re'-ah, and Jez-a-ni'-ah the son of Ho-sha'-iah, and all the people from the least even unto the greatest, came near."

"And said unto Jer-e-mi'-ah the prophet, Let, we beseech thee, our supplication be accepted before thee, and pray for us unto the LORD thy God, even for all this remnant; (for we are left but a few of many, as thine eyes do behold us:)"

"That the LORD thy God may shew us the way wherein we may walk, and the thing that we may do."

"Then Jer-e-mi'-ah the prophet said unto them, I have heard you; behold, I will pray unto the LORD your God according to your words; and it shall come to pass, that whatsoever thing the LORD shall answer you, I will declare it unto you; I will keep nothing back from you."

"Then they said to Jer-e-mi'-ah, The LORD be a true and faithful witness between us, if we do not even according to all things for the which the LORD thy God shall send thee to us."

"Whether it be good, or whether it be evil, we will obey the voice of the LORD our God, to whom we send thee; that it may be well with us, when we obey the voice of the LORD our God."

"And it came to pass after ten days, that the word of the LORD came unto Jer-e-mi'-ah."

"Then called he Jo-ha'-nan the son of Ka-re'-ah, and all the captains of the forces which were with him, and all the people from the least even to the greatest,"

"And said unto them, Thus saith the LORD, the God of Israel, unto whom ye sent me to present your supplication before him;"

"If ye will still abide in this land, then will I build you, and not pull you down, and I will plant you, and not pluck you up; for I repent me of the evil that I have done unto you."

"Be not afraid of the king of Babylon, of whom ye are afraid; be not afraid of him, saith the LORD; for I am with you to save you, and to deliver you from his hand."

"And I will shew mercies unto you, that he may have mercy upon you, and cause you to return to your own land."

"But if ye say, We will not dwell in this land, neither obey the voice of the LORD your God,"

"Saying, No; but we will go into the land of Egypt, where we shall see no war, nor hear the sound of the trumpet, nor have hunger of bread; and there will we dwell:"

"And now therefore hear the word of the LORD, ye remnant of Judah; Thus saith the LORD of hosts, the God of Israel; If ye wholly set your faces to enter into Egypt, and go to sojourn there;"

"Then it shall come to pass, that the sword, which ye feared, shall overtake you there in the land of Egypt, and the famine, whereof ye were afraid, shall follow close after you there in Egypt; and there ye shall die."

"So shall it be with all the men that set their faces to go into Egypt to sojourn there; they shall die by the sword, by the famine, and by the pestilence: and none of them shall remain or escape from the evil that I will bring upon them."

"For thus saith the LORD of hosts, the God of Israel; As mine anger and my fury hath been poured forth upon the inhabitants of Jerusalem; so shall my fury be poured forth upon you, when ye shall enter into Egypt: and ye shall be an execration, and an astonishment, and a curse, and a reproach; and ye shall see this place no more."

"The LORD hath said concerning you, O ye remnant of Judah; Go ye not into Egypt:

know certainly that I have admonished you this day."

"For ye dissembled in your hearts, when ye sent me unto the LORD your God, saying, Pray for us unto the LORD our God; and according unto all that the LORD our God shall say, so declare unto us, and we will do it."

"And now I have this day declared it to you; but ye have not obeyed the voice of the LORD your God, nor any thing for the which he hath sent me unto you."

"Now therefore know certainly that ye shall die by the sword, by the famine, and by the pestilence, in the place whither ye desire to go and to sojourn."

Jeremiah teaches about the relationship between our obedience and the protection of God.

(Jeremiah 42:1-22)

PROMISE FROM GOD

"For he shall give his angels charge over thee, to keep thee in all thy ways."

(Psalm 91:11)

PROVISION

62. What does it mean to trust God's provision?

"AND Joshua rose early in the morning; and they removed from Shit'-tim, and came to Jordan, he and all the children of Israel, and lodged there before they passed over."

"And it came to pass after three days, that the officers went through the host;"

"And they commanded the people, saying, When ye see the ark of the covenant of the LORD your God and the priests the Levites bearing it, then ye shall remove from your place, and go after it."

"Yet there shall be a space between you and it, about two thousand cubits by measure: come not near unto it, that ye may know the way by which ye must go: for ye have not passed this way heretofore."

"And Joshua said unto the people, Sanctify yourselves: for to morrow the LORD will do wonders among you."

"And Joshua spake unto the priests, saying, Take up the ark of the covenant, and pass over before the people. And they took up the ark of the covenant, and went before the people."

"And the LORD said unto Joshua, This day will I begin to magnify thee in the sight of all Israel, that they may know that, as I was with Moses, so I will be with thee."

"And thou shalt command the priests that bear the ark of the covenant, saying, When ye are come to the brink of the water of Jordan, ye shall stand still in Jordan."

"And Joshua said unto the children of Israel, Come hither, and hear the words of the LORD your God."

"And Joshua said, Hereby ye shall know that the living God is among you, and that he will without fail drive out from before you the Ca'-naan-ites, and the Hit'-tites, and the Hi'-vites, and the Per'-iz-zites, and the Gir'-ga-shites, and the Am'-or-ites, and the Jeb'-u-sites."

We most often experience the provision of God when we are following him in obedience.

(Joshua 3:1-10)

"Then said the LORD unto Moses, Behold, I will rain bread from heaven for you; and the people shall go out and gather a certain rate every day, that I may prove them, whether they will walk in my law, or no."

"And it shall come to pass, that on the sixth day they shall prepare that which they bring in; and it shall be twice as much as they gather daily."

"And Moses and Aaron said unto all the children of Israel, At even, then ye shall know that the Lord hath brought you out from the land of Egypt:"

"And in the morning, then ye shall see the glory of the LORD; for that he heareth your murmurings against the LORD: and what are we, that ye murmur against us?"

"And Moses said, This shall be, when the LORD shall give you in the evening flesh to eat, and in the morning bread to the full; for that the LORD heareth your murmurings which ye murmur against him: and what are we? your murmurings are not against us but against the LORD."

"And Moses spake unto Aaron, Say unto all the congregation of the children of Israel, Come near before the LORD: for he hath heard your murmurings."

"And it came to pass, as Aaron spake unto the whole congregation of the children of Israel, that they looked toward the wilderness, and, behold, the glory of the LORD appeared in the cloud."

"And the LORD spake unto Moses, saying,"

I have heard the murmurings of the children of Israel; speak unto them, saying, At even ye shall eat flesh, and in the morning ye shall be filled with bread; and ye shall know that I am the LORD your God."

"And it came to pass, that at even quails came up, and covered the camp; and in the morning the dew lay round about the host."

"And when the dew that lay was gone up, behold, upon the face of the wilderness there lay a small round thing, as small as the hoar frost on the ground."

"And when the children of Israel saw it, they said one to another, It is man'-na: for they wist not what it was. And Moses said unto them, This is the bread which the LORD hath given you to eat."

"This is the thing which the LORD hath commanded, Gather of it every man according to his eating, an o'-mer for every man, according to the number of your persons; take ye every man for them which are in his tents."

"And the children of Israel did so, and gathered, some more, some less."

"And when they did mete it with an o'-mer, he that gathered much had nothing over, and he that gathered little had no lack; they gathered every man according to his eating."

"And Moses said, Let no man leave of it till the morning."

"Notwithstanding they hearkened not unto Moses; but some of them left of it until morning, and it bred worms, and stank: and Moses was wroth with them."

"And they gathered it every morning, every man according to his eating: and when the sun waxed hot, it melted."

"And it came to pass, that on the sixth day they gathered twice as much bread, two o'-mers for one man: and all the rulers of the congregation came and told Moses."

"And he said unto them, This is that which the LORD hath said, To morrow is the rest of the holy sabbath unto the LORD; bake that which ye will bake to day, and seethe that ye will seethe; and that which remaineth over lay up for you to be kept until the morning."

"And they laid it up till the morning, as Moses bade: and it did not stink, neither was there any worm therein."

"And Moses said, Eat that to day; for to day is a sabbath unto the LORD: to day ye shall not find it in the field."

"Six days ye shall gather it; but on the seventh day, which is the sabbath, in it there shall be none."

"And it came to pass, that there went out some of the people on the seventh day for to gather, and they found none."

"And the LORD said unto Moses, How long refuse ye to keep my commandments and my laws?"

"See, for that the LORD hath given you the sabbath, therefore he giveth you on the sixth day the bread of two days; abide ye every man in his place, let no man go out of his place, on the seventh day."

"So the people rested on the seventh day."

God accommodated the day by day needs of his people. When they struggled, it was on the grounds that greed and disobedience led to problems in distribution.

(Exodus 16:4-30)

"According as his divine power hath given unto us all things that pertain unto life and godliness, through the knowledge of him that hath called us to glory and virtue:"

"Whereby are given unto us exceeding great and precious promises: that by these ye might be partakers of the divine nature, having escaped the corruption that is in the world through lust."

God has provided resources from his own character to those who seek him.

(II Peter 1:3, 4)

"And Jesus said unto them, I am the bread of life: he that cometh to me shall never hunger; and he that believeth on me shall never thirst."

Our deepest hunger is met not by bread but by the filling of our hearts with the love and power of Jesus Christ himself.

(John 6:35)

"To the praise of the glory of his grace, wherein he hath made us accepted in the beloved."

"In whom we have redemption through his blood, the forgiveness of sins, according to the riches of his grace;"

"Wherein he hath abounded toward us in all wisdom and prudence;"

Through the riches of his grace God has provided for our greatest need-forgiveness of sin and salvation in Jesus Christ.

(Ephesians 1:6-8)

PROMISE FROM GOD

"But my God shall supply all your need according to his riches in glory by Christ Jesus."

(Philippians 4:19)

PUNISHMENT

63. Why are the punishments in the Old Testament so severe?

"And God said unto the serpent, Because thou hast done this, thou art cursed above all cattle, and above every beast of the field; upon thy belly shalt thou go, and dust shalt thou eat all the days of thy life:"

"And I will put enmity between thee and the woman, and between thy seed and her seed;

it shall bruise thy head, and thou shalt bruise his heel."

(Genesis 3:14, 15)

"And the Lord said unto Cain, Where is Abel thy brother? And he said, I know not: Am I my brother's keeper?"

"And he said, What hast thou done? The voice of thy brother's blood crieth unto me from the ground."

"And now art thou cursed from the earth, which hath opened her mouth to receive thy brother's blood from thy hand;"

"When thou tillest the ground, it shall not henceforth yield unto thee her strength; a fugitive and a vagabond shalt thou be in the earth."

"And Cain said unto the LORD, My punishment is greater than I can bear."

"Behold, thou hast driven me out this day from the face of the earth; and from thy face shall I be hid; and I shall be a fugitive and a vagabond in the earth; and it shall come to pass, that every one that findeth me shall slay me."

"And the LORD said unto him, Therefore whosoever slayeth Cain, vengeance shall be taken on him sevenfold. And the LORD set a mark upon Cain, lest any finding him should kill him."

From now on you will be a homeless fugitive on the earth.

(Genesis 4:9-16)

"AND THE LORD spake unto Moses, saying,"

"Again, thou shalt say to the children of Israel, Whosoever he be of the children of Israel, or of the strangers that sojourn in Israel, that giveth any of his seed unto Mo'-lech; he shall surely be put to death: the people of the land shall stone him with stones."

"And I will set my face against that man, and will cut him off from among his people; because he hath given of his seed unto Mo'-lech, to defile my sanctuary, and to profane my holy name."

"And if the people of the land do any ways hide their eyes from the man, when he giveth of his seed unto Mo'-lech, and kill him not:"

"Then I will set my face against that man, and against his family, and will cut him off, and all that go a whoring after him, to commit whoredom with Mo'-lech, from among their people."

"And the soul that turneth after such as have familiar spirits, and after wizards, to go a whoring after them, I will even set my face against that soul, and will cut him off from among his people."

"Sanctify yourselves therefore, and be ye holy: for I am the LORD your God."

"And ye shall keep my statutes, and do them: I am the LORD which sanctify you."

"For every one that curseth his father or mother shall be surely put to death: he hath cursed his father or his mother; his blood shall be upon him."

"And the man that committeth adultery with another man's wife, even he that committeth adultery with his neighbour's wife, the adulterer and the adultress shall surely be put to death."

"And the man that lieth with his father's wife hath uncovered his father's nakedness:

both of them shall surely be put to death; their blood shall be upon them."

"And if a man lie with is daughter in law, both of them shall surely be put to death; they have wrought confusion; their blood shall be upon them."

"If a man also lie with mankind, as he lieth with a woman, both of them have committed an abomination: they shall surely be put to death; their blood shall be upon them."

"And if a man take a wife and her mother, it is wickedness: they shall be burnt with fire, both he and they; that there be no wickedness among you."

"And if a man lie with a beast, he shall surely be put to death: and ye shall slay the beast."

"And if a woman approach unto any beast, and lie down thereto, thou shalt kill the woman, and the beast: they shall surely be put to death; their blood shall be upon them."

"And if a man shall take his sister, his father's daughter, or his mother's daughter, and see her nakedness, and she see his nakedness; it is a wicked thing; and they shall be cut off in the sight of their people: he hath uncovered his sister's nakedness; he shall bear his iniquity."

"And if a man shall lie with a woman having her sickness, and shall uncover her nakedness; he hath discovered her fountain, and she hath uncovered the fountain of her blood: and both of them shall be cut off from among their people."

"And thou shalt not uncover the nakedness of thy mother's sister, nor of thy father's sister: for he uncovereth his near kin: they shall bear their iniquity."

"And if a man shall lie with his uncle's wife, he hath uncovered his uncle's nakedness:

they shall bear their sin; they shall die childless."

"And if a man shall take his brother's wife, it is an unclean thing: he hath uncovered his brother's nakedness; they shall be childless."

"Ye shall therefore keep all my statutes, and all my judgments, and do them: that the land, whither I bring you to dwell therein, spue you not out."

"And ye shall not walk in the manners of the nation, which I cast out before you: for they committed all these things, and therefore I abhorred them."

"But I have said unto you, Ye shall inherit their land, and I will give it unto you to possess it, a land that floweth with milk and honey: I am the LORD your God, which have separated you from other people."

"Ye therefore put difference between clean beasts and unclean, and between unclean fowls and clean: and ye shall not make your souls abominable by beast, or by fowl, or by any manner of living thing that creepeth on the ground, which I have separated from you as unclean."

"And ye shall be holy unto me: for I the LORD am holy, and have severed you from other people, that ye should be mine."

"A man also or woman that hath a familiar spirit, or that is a wizard, shall surely be put to death: they shall stone them with stones: their blood shall be upon them."

The serpent was punished for tempting Eve into sin; Cain's punishment was living with the guilt of killing his brother. The seriousness of these punishments was intended to present for God's people the seriousness of sin.

(Leviticus 20:1-27)

64. Does God discipline us today? How?

"If ye endure chastening, God dealeth with you as with sons; for what son is he whom the father chasteneth not?"

"But if ye be without chastisement, whereof all are partakers, then are ye bastards, and not sons."

"Furthermore we have had fathers of our flesh which corrected us, and we gave them reverence: shall we not much rather be in subjection unto the Father of spirits, and live?"

"For they verily for a few days chastened us after their own pleasure; but he for our profit, that we might be partakers of his holiness."

"Now no chastening for the present seemeth to be joyous, but grievous; nevertheless afterward it yieldeth the peaceable fruit of righteousness unto them which are exercised thereby."

Be that as it may, God's discipline is in every case right and good because it means we will share in his holiness.

God disciplines us as a loving Father, by both consequences and rebuke. His desire is consistently to bring us back to him, not to humiliate or hurt us.

(Hebrews 12:7-11)

"For the wrath of God is revealed from heaven against all ungodliness and unrighteousness of men, who hold the truth in unrighteousness;"

"Because that which may be know of God's manifest in them; for God hath shewed it unto them."

"For the invisible things of him from the creation of the world are clearly seen, being understood by the things that are made, even his eternal power and Godhead; so that they are without excuse:"

"Because that, when they knew God, they glorified him not as God, neither were thankful; but became vain in their imaginations, and their foolish heart was darkened."

"Professing themselves to be wise, they became fools,"

"And changed the glory of the uncorruptible God into an image made like to corruptible man, and to birds, and fourfooted beasts, and creeping things."

"Wherefore God also gave them up to uncleanness through the lusts of their own hearts, to dishonour their own bodies between themselves:"

"Who changed the truth of God into a lie, and worshipped and served the creature more than the Creator, who is blessed for ever. A-men'."

"For this cause God gave them up unto vile affections: for even their women did change the natural use into that which is against nature:"

"And likewise also the men, leaving the natural use of the woman, burned in their lust one toward another; men with men working that which is unseemly, and receiving in themselves that recompence of their error which was meet."

"And even as they did not like to retain God in their knowledge, God gave them over to a reprobate mind, to do those things which are not convenient;"

Being filled with all unrighteousness, fornication, wickedness, covetousness, maliciousness; full of envy, murder, debate, deceit, malignity; whisperers,"

"Backbiters, haters of God, despiteful, proud, boasters, inventors of evil things, disobedient to parents,"

"Without understanding, covenant breakers, without natural affection, implacable, unmerciful:"

"Who knowing the judgment of God, that they which commit such things are worthy of death, not only do the same, but have pleasure in them that do them."

That is why God abandoned them to shameful desires.

God gives sinners over to the consequences of their own behavior, especially when their sin is intentional and deliberate.

(Romans 1:18-32)

65. Will we be punished for our sins?

"For, behold, the LORD cometh out of his place to punish the inhabitants of the earth for their iniquity; the earth also shall disclose her blood, and shall no more cover her slain."

Judgment and punishment are promised for all sin.

(Isaiah 26:21)

"He was taken from prison and from judgment: and who shall declare his generation? For he was cut off out of the land of the living; for the transgression of my people was he stricken."

"But who among the people realized that he was dying for their sins-that he was suffering their punishment?"

(Isaiah 53:8)

"And they cried with a loud voice, saying, How long, O Lord, holy and true, dost thou not judge and avenge our blood on them that dwell on the earth?"

(Revelation 6:10)

"Wherein they think it strange that ye run not with them to the same excess of riot, speaking evil of you:"

"Who shall give account to him that is ready to judge the quick and the dead."

Judgment will surely come upon all who reject Christ.

(I Peter 4:4, 5)

PROMISE FROM GOD

"For all have sinned, and come short of the glory of God;"

"Being justified freely by his grace through the redemption that is in Christ Jesus:"

(Romans 3:23-28)

PURPOSE

66. How can I know God's purpose for my life?

"Then the children of Judah came unto Joshua in Gil'-gal: and Caleb the son of Je-phun'-neh the Ken'-ez-ite said unto him, Thou knowest the thing that the LORD said unto Moses the man of God concerning me and thee in Ka'-desh-bar'-ne-a."

"Forty years old was I when Moses the servant of the LORD sent me from Ka'-desh-bar'-ne-a to espy out the land; and I brought him word again as it was in mine heart."

"Nevertheless my brethren that went up with me made the heart of the people melt; but I wholly followed the LORD my God."

"And Moses sware on that day, saying, Surely the land whereon thy feet have trodden shall be thine inheritance, and thy children's for ever, because thou hast wholly followed the LORD thy God."

"And now, behold, the LORD hath kept me alive, as he said, these forty and five years, even since the LORD spake this word unto Moses, while the children of Israel wandered in the wilderness: and now, lo, I am this day fourscore and five years old."

Dr. John Thomas Wylie

"As yet I am as strong this day as I was in the day that Moses sent me: as my strength was then, even so is my strength now, for war, both to go out, and to come in."

"Now therefore give me this mountain, whereof the LORD spake in that day; for thou heardest in that day how the An'-a-kims were there, and that the cities were great and fenced: if so be the LORD will be with me, then I shall be able to drive them out,"

"And Joshua blessed him, and gave Caleb the son of Je-phun'-neh He'-bron for an inheritance."

"He'-bron therefore became the inheritance of Caleb the son of Je-phun'-neh the Ken'-ez-ite unto this day, because that he wholly followed the LORD God of Israel."

"And the name of He'-bron before was Kir'-jath-ar'-ba; which Ar'-ba was a great man among the An'-a-kims. And the land had rest from war."

But if the LORD is with me, I will drive them out of the land, just as the LORD said…

A vision of God's future allowed Caleb to see his own purpose and not the strength of his enemies.

(Joshua 14:6-15)

"And David rose up early in the morning, and left the sheep with a keeper, and took, and went, as Jesse had commanded him; and he came to the trench, as the host was going forth to the fight, and shouted for the battle."

"For Israel and the Phi-lis'-tines had put the battle in array, army against army."

"And David left his carriage in the hand of the keeper of the carriage, and ran into the army, and came and saluted his brethren."

"And as he talked with them, behold, there came up the champion, the Phi-lis'-tine of Gath, Go-li-ath by name, out of the armies of the Phi-lis'-tines, and spake according to the same words: and David heard them."

"And all the men of Israel, when they saw the man, fled from him, and were sore afraid."

"And the men of Israel said, Have ye seen this man that is come up? Surely to defy Israel is he come up:

and it shall be, that the man who killeth him, the king will enrich him with great riches, and will give him his daughter, and make his father's house free in Israel."

"And David spake to the men that stood by him, saying, What shall be done to the man that killeth this Phi-lis'-tine, and taketh away the reproach from Israel? For who is this uncircumcised Phi-lis'-tine, that he should defy the armies of the living God?"

"And the people answered him after this manner, saying, So shall it be done to the man that killeth him."

"And E-li'-ab his eldest brother heard when he spake unto the men; and E-li'-ab's anger was kindled against David, and he said, Why camest thou down hither? and with whom hast thou left those few sheep in the wilderness? I know thy pride, and the naughtiness of thine heart; for thou art come down that thou mightest see the battle."

"And David said, What have I now done? Is there not a cause?"

"And he turned from him toward another, and spake after the same manner: and the people answered him again after the former manner."

"And when the words were heard which David spake, they rehearsed them before Saul:

and he sent for him."

"And David said to Saul, Let no man's heart fail because of him; thy servant will go and fight with this Phi-lis'-tine."

"And Saul said to David, Thou art not able to go against this Phi-lis'-tine to fight with him: for thou art but a youth, and he a man of war from his youth."

"And David said unto Saul, Thy servant kept his father's sheep, and there came a lion, and a bear, and took a lamb out of the flock:"

"And I went out after him, and smote him, and delivered it out of his mouth: and when he arose against me, I caught him by his beard, and smote him, and slew him."

"Thy servant slew both the lion and the bear: and this uncircumcised Phi-lis'-tine shall be as one of them, seeing he hath defied the armies of the living God."

"David said moreover, The LORD that delivered me out of the paw of the lion, and out of the paw of the bear, he will deliver me out of the hand of this

Phi-lis'-tine. And Saul said unto David, Go, and the LORD be with thee."

While others saw a fearsome giant, David saw an opportunity for God's mighty work.

(I Samuel 17:20-37)

"Then said I unto them, Ye see the distress that we are in, how Jerusalem lieth waste, and the gates thereof are burned with fire; come, and let us build up the wall of Jerusalem, that we be no more a reproach."

"Then I told them of the hand of my God which was good upon me; as also the king's words that he had spoken unto me. And they said, Let us rise up and build. So they strengthened their hands for this good work."

Nehemiah's passion to rebuild the walls of Jerusalem was rooted in God's purposes for his people.

(Nehemiah 2:17, 18)

"According to my earnest expectation and my hope, that in nothing I shall be ashamed, but that with all boldness, as always, so now also whether it be by life, or by death."

"For to me to live is Christ, and to die is gain."

"But if I live in the flesh, this is the fruit of my labour: yet what I shall choose I wot not."

"For I am in a strait betwixt two, having a desire to depart, and to be with Christ; which is far better:"

"Nevertheless to abide in the flesh is more needful for you."

(Philippians 1:20-24)

"Yea doubtless, and I count all things but loss for the excellency of the knowledge of Christ Jesus my Lord: for whom I have suffered the loss of all things, and do count them but dung, that I may win Christ."

"That I may know him, and the power of his resurrection, and the fellowship of his sufferings, being made conformable unto his death;"

"Not as though I had already attained, either were already perfect: but I follow after, if that I may apprehend that for which also I am apprehended of Christ Jesus."

"Brethren, I count not myself to have apprehended: but this one thing I do, forgetting those things which are behind, and reaching forth unto those things which are before,"

"I press toward the mark for the prize of the high calling of God in Christ Jesus."

Paul's great purpose, whether by life or death, was to win others to Christ.

(Philippians 3:8-14)

PROMISE FROM GOD

"Not as though I had already attained, either were already perfect: but I follow after, if that I may apprehend that for which also I am apprehended of Christ Jesus."

"Brethren, I count not myself to have apprehended: but this one thing I do, forgetting those things which are behind, and reaching forth unto those things which are before,"

"I press toward the mark for the prize of the high calling of God in Christ Jesus."

I don't mean to say I have already achieved these things or that I have already reached perfection! But I keep working toward that day when I will finally be all that Christ Jesus saved me for and wants me to be. No, dear friends, I am still not all I should be, but I am focusing all my energies on this one thing: Forgetting the past and looking forward to what lies ahead. I strain to reach the end of the race and receive the prize for which God, through Christ Jesus is calling us up to heaven.

(Philippians 3:12-14)

QUITTING

67. How can I keep going when I feel like quitting?

"And now, behold, I go bound in the spirit unto Jerusalem, not knowing the things that shall befall me there;"

"Save that the Holy Ghost witnesseth in every city, saying that bonds and afflictions abide me."

"But none of these things move me, neither count I my life dear unto myself, so that I might finish my course with joy, and the ministry, which I have received of the Lord Jesus, to testify the gospel of the grace of God."

Paul faced unimaginable hardship yet finished the course.

(Acts 20:22-24)

"But we have this treasure in earthen vessels, that the excellency of the power may be of God, and not of us."

"We are troubled on every side, yet not distressed; we are perplexed, but not in despair;"

"Persecuted, but not forsaken; cast down, but not destroyed;"

"Always bearing about in the body the dying of the Lord Jesus, that the life also of Jesus might be made manifest in our body."

Even in the midst of suffering, believers can find strength to endure for Christ.

(II Corinthians 4:7-10)

"I have fought a good fight, I have finished my course, I have kept the faith:"

"Henceforth there is laid up for me a crown of righteousness, which the Lord, the righteous judge, shall give me at that day: and not to me only, but unto all them also that love his appearing."

I have fought a good fight, I have finished the race, and I have remained faithful.

(II Timothy 4:7, 8)

"And let us not be weary in well doing: for in due season we shall reap, if we faint not."

We avoid discouragement by keeping our eyes on the goal and reward of heaven.

(Galatians 6:9)

PROMISE FROM GOD

"And ye shall be hated of all men for my name's sake: but he that endureth to the end shall be saved."

(Matthew 10:22)

REBELLION

68. What does it mean to rebel against God?

"And I will utter my judgments against them touching all their wickedness, who have forsaken me, and have burned incense unto other gods, and worshipped the works of their own hands."

(Jeremiah 1:16)

"For where your treasure is, there will your heart be also."

We rebel against God whenever we give our devotion to other things.

(Matthew 6:21)

"And the children of Israel did evil in the sight of the LORD, and served Ba'-a-lim:"

"And they forsook the LORD God of their fathers, which brought them out of the land of Egypt, and followed other gods, of the gods of the people that were round about them, and bowed themselves unto them, and provoked the LORD to anger."

"And they forsook the LORD, and served Ba'-al and Ash'-ta-roth."

"And the anger of the LORD was hot against Israel, and he delivered them into the hands of spoilers that spoiled them, and he sold them into the hands of their enemies round about, so that they could not any longer stand before their enemies."

When our rebellion leads to false worship, we are in danger of destruction.

(Judges 2:11-14)

"But your iniquities have separated between you and your God, and your sins have hid his face from you, that he will not hear."

Your sins have cut you off from God.

(Isaiah 59:2)

"Whosoever committeth sin transgresseth also the law: for sin is the transgression of the law."

Those who sin are opposed to the law of God.

Sin is rebellion to God, wanting to do things our way. At the point when we defy (rebel against) God we become separated from him.

(I John 3:4)

"If ye will fear the LORD, and serve him, and obey his voice, and not rebel against the commandment of the LORD then shall both ye and also the king that reigneth over you continue following the LORD your God:"

"But if ye will not obey the voice of the LORD, but rebel against the commandment of the LORD, then shall the hand of the LORD be against you, as it was against your fathers."

Rebellion is refusing to listen to and obey God.

(I Samuel 12:14, 15)

"But the house of Israel rebelled against me in the wilderness: they walked not in my statutes, and they despised my judgments, which if a man do, he shall even live in them; and my sabbaths they greatly polluted: then I said, I would pour out my fury upon them in the wilderness, to consume them."

Some of the time our disobedience can be obstinate (stubborn) to such an extent that we will not obey in any event, even when obedience means our very life.

(Ezekiel 20:13)

"Wherefore (as the Holy Ghost saith, TO DAY IF YE WILL HEAR HIS VOICE,"

"HARDEN NOT YOUR HEARTS, AS IN THE PROVOCATION, IN THE DAY OF TEMPTATION IN THE WILDERNESS:"

"WHEN YOUR FATHERS TEMPTED ME, PROVED ME, AND SAW MY WORKS FORTY YEARS."

"WHEREFORE I WAS GRIEVED WITH THAT GENERATION, AND SAID, THEY DO ALWAY ERR IN THEIR HEART; AND THEY HAVE NOT KNOWN MY WAYS."

"SO I SWARE IN MY WRATH, THEY SHALL NOT ENTER INTO MY REST.)"

"Take heed, brethren, lest there be in any of you an evil heart of unbelief, in departing from the living God."

:But exhort one another daily, while it is called To day; lest any of you be hardened through the deceitfulness of sin."

"For we are made partakers of Christ, if we hold the beginning of our confidence stedfast unto the end;"

"While it is said, TO DAY IF YE WILL HEAR HIS VOICE, HARDEN NOT YOUR HEARTS, AS IN THE PROVOCATION."

The ultimate spiritual rebellion is refusing to accept the gracious offer of salvation through Jesus Christ.

(Hebrews 3:7-15)

"WHEN Israel was a child, then I loved him, and called my son out of Egypt."

"As they called them, so they went from them: they sacrificed unto Ba'-al-im, and burned incense to graven images."

"I taught E'-phra-im also to go, taking them by their arms; but they knew not that I healed them."

"I drew them with cords of a man, with bands of love: and I was to them as they that take off the yoke on their jaws, and I laid meat unto them."

"He shall not return into the land of Egypt, but the Assyrian shall be his king, because they refused to return."

"And the sword shall abide on his cities, and shall consume his branches, and devour them, because of their own counsels."

"And my people are bent to backsliding from me: though they called them to the most High, none at all would exalt him."

"How shall I give thee up, E'-phra-im? how shall I deliver thee, Israel? how shall I set thee as Ze-bo'-lim? mine heart is turned within me, my repenting are kindled together."

"I will not execute the fierceness of mine anger, I will not return to destroy E'-phra-im: for I am God, and not man; the Holy One in the midst of thee: and I will not enter into the city."

"They shall walk after the LORD: he shall roar like a lion: when he shall roar, then the children shall tremble from the west."

"They shall tremble as a bird out of Egypt, and as a dove out of the land of Assyria: and I will place them in their houses, saith the LORD."

Regardless of how far the rebel strays, God despite everything loves that person (him or her) with an everlasting love.

(Hosea 11:1-11)

69. Isn't a certain amount of rebellion to be expected-for example with teenagers?

"AND it came to pass after this, that Ab'-sa-lom prepared him chariots and horses, and fifty men to run before him."

"And Ab'-sa-lom rose up early, and stood beside the way of the gate: and it was so, that when any man that had a controversy came to the king for judgment, then Ab'-sa-lom called unto him, and said, Of what city art thou? And he said, Thy servant is of one of the tribe of Israel."

"And Ab'-sa-lom said unto him, See, thy matters are good and right; but there is no man deputed of the king to hear thee."

"Ab'-sa-lom said moreover, Oh that I were made judge in the land, that every man which hath any suit or cause might come unto me, and I would do him justice!"

"And it was so, that when any man came nigh to him to do him obeisance, he put forth his hand, and took him and kissed him."

"And on this manner did Ab'-sa-lom to all Israel that came to the king for judgment: so Ab'-sa-lom stole the hearts of the men of Israel."

"And it came to pass after forty years, that Ab'-sa-lom said unto the king, I pray thee, let me go and pay my vow, which I have vowed unto the LORD, in He'-bron."

"For thy servant vowed a vow while I abode at Ge'-shur in Syria, sayhing, If the LORD shall bring me again indeed to Jerusalem, then I will serve the LORD."

"And the king said unto him, Go in peace. So he arose, and went to He'-bron."

"But Ab'-sa-lom sent spies throughout all the tribes of Israel, saying, As soon as ye hear the sound of the trumpet, then ye shall say, Ab'-sa-lom reigneth in He'-bron."

"And with Ab'-sa-lom went two hundred men out of Jerusalem, that were called; and they went in their simplicity, and they knew not any thing."

"And Ab'-sa-lom sent for A-hith'-o-phel the Gi'-lo-nite, David's counsellor, from his city, even from Gi'-loh, while he offered sacrifices. And the conspiracy was strong; for the people increased continually with Ab'-sa-lom."

"And there came a messenger to David, saying, The hearts of the men of Israel are after Ab'-sa-lom."

"And David said unto all his servants that were with him at Jerusalem, Arise, and let us flee; for we shall not else escape from Ab'-sa-lom: make speed to depart, lest he overtake us suddenly, and bring evil upon us, and smite the city with the edge of the sword."

"And the king's servants said unto the king, Behold, thy servants are ready to do whatsoever my lord the king shall appoint."

"And the king went forth, and all his household after him. And the king left ten women, which were concubines, to keep the house."

"And the king went forth, and all the people after him, and tarried in a place that was far off."

"And all his servants passed on beside him; and all the Cher'-e-thites, and all the Pel'-e-thites, and all the Git'-tites, six hundred men which came after him from Gath, passed on before the king."

"Unto whom Davide said, If thou passest on with me, then thou shalt be a burden unto me:"

The story of Absalom and David is a classic and heartbreaking story of the rebellion of son against father.

(II Samuel 15:1-18, 33)

"CHILDREN, obey your parents in the Lord: for this is right."

"HONOUR THY FATHER AND MOTHER; which is the first commandment with promise;"

"THAT IT MAY BE WELL WITH THEE, AND THOU MAYEST LIVE LONG ON THE EARTH."

"And, ye fathers, provoke not your children to wrath; but bring them up in the nurture and admonition of the Lord."

Authority without loving relationship always provokes rebellion.

(Ephesians 6:1-4)

70. Is rebellion ever good?

"FORASMUCH then as Christ hath suffered for us in the flesh, arm yourselves likewise with the same mind: for he that hath suffered in the flesh hath ceased from sin;"

"That he no longer should live the rest of his time in the flesh to the lusts of men, but to the will of God."

"For the time past of our life may suffice us to have wrought the will of the Gentiles, when we walked in lasciviousness, lusts, excess of wine, revellings, banquetings, and abominaable idolatries:"

"Wherein they think it strange that ye run out with them to the same excess of riot, speaking evil of you:"

"Who shall give account to him that is ready to judge the quick and the dead."

When constrained (under pressure) to take an interest or participate in sinful activities, the Christian is to rebel against the crowd.

(I Peter 4:1-5)

"And Jesus went into the temple of God, and cast out all them that sold and bought in the temple, and overthrew the tables of the moneychangers, and the seats of them that sold doves,"

"And said unto them, It is written, MY HOUSE SHALL BE CALLED THE HOUSE OF PRAYER; but ye have made it a DEN OF THIEVES."

Here, Jesus himself rebelled against the systematic corruption of the Temple.

(Matthew 21:12, 13)

PROMISE FROM GOD

"Return, ye backsliding children, and I will heal your backslidings. Behold, we come unto thee; for thou art the LORD our God."

"My wayward children," says the LORD, "return to me, and I will heal your wayward hearts." "Indeed, we will come," the people answer, "for you are the LORD our God."

(Jeremiah 3:22)

RECONCILIATION

71. What does it mean to be reconciled to God?

"And all things are of God, who hath reconciled us to himself by Jesus Christ, and hath given to us the ministry of reconciliation:"

"To wit, that God was in Christ, reconciling the world unto himself, not imputing their trespasses unto them; and hath committed unto us the word of reconciliation."

"Now then we are ambassadors for Christ, as though God did beseech you by us: we pray you in Christ's stead, be ye reconciled to God."

"For he hath made him to be sin for us, who knew no sin; that we might be made the righteousness of God in him."

(II Corinthians 5:18-21)

"Wherefore remember, that ye being in time past Gentiles in the flesh, who are called Uncircumcision by that which is called the Circumcision in the flesh made by hands;"

"That at that time ye were without Christ, being aliens from the commonwealth of Israel, and strangers from the covenants of promise, having no hope, and without God in the world:"

"But now in Christ Jesus ye who sometimes were far off are made nigh by the blood of Christ."

"For he is our peace, who hath made both one, and hath broken down the middle wall of partition between us;"

"Having abolished in his flesh the enmity, even the law of commandments contained in ordinances; for to make in himself of twain one new man, so making peace;"

"And that he might reconcile both unto God in one body by the cross, having slain the enmity thereby:"

"And came and preached peace to you which were afar off, and to them that were nigh."

"For through him we both have access by one Spirit unto the Father."

"Now therefore ye are no more strangers and foreigners, but fellow citizens with the saints, and of the household of God;"

"And are built upon the foundation of the apostles and prophets, Jesus Christ himself being the chief corner stone;"

"In whom all the building fitly framed together groweth unto an holy temple in the Lord:"

Though you once were far away from God, now you have been brought near to him because of the blood of Christ...

Reconciliation begins with an acknowledgment that without Christ we are lost and separated from God.

(Ephesians 2:11-21)

"THEREFORE being justified by faith, we have peace with God through our Lord Jesus Christ;"

"By whom also we have access by faith into this grace wherein we stand, and rejoice in hope of the glory of God."

Reconciliation with God comes through faith and brings peace.

(Romans 5:1, 2)

72. How can I mend a broken relationship with a friend?

"Forbearing one another, and forgiving one another, if any man have a quarrel against any; even as Christ forgave you, so also do ye."

You must make allowance for each other's faults and forgive the person who offends you.

(Colossians 3:13)

"I beseech thee for my son O-nes'-i-mus, whom I have begotten in my bonds:"

"Which in time past was to thee unprofitable, but now profitable to thee and to me:"

"Whom I have sent again: thou therefore receive him, that is, mine own bowels:"

Reconciliation requires someone to take a first step of kindness. It requires us to look at a person in a new way.

(Philemon 1:10-12)

PROMISE FROM GOD

"Come now, and let us reason together, saith the LORD: though your sins be as scarlet, they shall be as white as snow; though they be red like crimson, they shall be as wool."

(Isaiah 1:18)

REGRETS

73. How can I deal with the regrets of my life?

"HAVE mercy upon me, O God, according to thy lovingkindness; according unto the multitude of thy tender mercies blot out my transgressions."

"Wash me thoroughly from mine iniquity, and cleanse me from my sin."

"For I acknowledge my transgressions: and my sin is ever before me."

"Against thee, thee only, have I sinned, and done this evil in thy sight: that thou mightest be justified when thou speakest, and be clear when thou judgest."

"Behold, I was shapen in iniquity; and in sin did my mother conceive me." "Behold, thou desirest truth in the inward parts: and in the hidden part thou shalt make me to know wisdom."

"Purge me with hyssop, and I shall be clean: wash me, and I shall be whiter than snow."

"Make me to hear joy and gladness; that the bones which thou hast broken may rejoice."

"Hide my face from my sins, and blot out all mine iniquities."

"Create in me a clean heart, O God; and renew a right spirit within me."

"Cast me not away from thy presence; and take not the holy spirit from me."

"Restore unto me the joy of thy salvation; and uphold me with thy free spirit."

"Then will I teach transgressors thy ways; and sinners shall be converted unto thee."

"Deliver me from bloodguiltiness, O God, thou God of my salvation: and my tongue shall sing aloud of thy righteousness."

"O Lord, open thou my lips; and my mouth shall shew forth thy praise."

Regrets caused by sin are cleansed through heartfelt confession, forgiveness, and repentance.

(Psalm 51:1-15)

"Yet will I leave a remnant, that ye may have some that shall escape the sword among the nations, when ye shall be scattered through the countries."

"And they that escape of you shall remember me among the nations whither they shall be carried captives, because I am broken with their whorish heart, which hath departed from me, and with their eyes, which go a whoring after idols: and they shall loathe themselves for the evils which they have committed in all their abominations."

"And they shall know that I am the LORD, and that I have not said in vain that I would do this evil unto them."

"Thus saith the Lord God; Smite with thine hand, and stamp with thy foot, and say, Alas for all the evil abominations of the house of Israel! For they shall fall by the sword by the famine, and by the pestilence."

God some of the time uses brokenness and remorse to bring true repentance.

(Ezekiel 6:8-11)

74. How can I avoid regrets in the future?

"Then Judas, which had betrayed him, when he saw that he was condemned, repented himself, and brought again the thirty pieces of silver to the chief priests and elders,"

"Saying, I have sinned in that I have betrayed the innocent blood. And they said, What is that to us? See thou to that."

"And he cast down the pieces of silver in the temple, and departed, and went and hanged himself."

"And the chief priests took the silver pieces, and said, It is not lawful for to put them into the treasury, because it is the price of blood."

"And they took counsel, and bought with them the potter's field, to bury strangers in."

"Wherefore that field was called, The field of blood, unto this day."

"Then was fulfilled that which was spoken by Jeremy the prophet, saying, AND THEY TOOK THE THIRTY PIECES OF SILVER, THE PRICE OF HIM THAT WAS VALUED, whom they of the children of Israel did value;"

"AND GAVE THEM FOR THE POTTER'S FIELD, AS THE LORD APPOINTED ME.

When Judas, who had betrayed him, realized that Jesus had been condemned to die, he was filled with remorse...

Judas's self-destructive regrets were caused by a combination of selfishness and a failure to consider the full consequences of his decision.

`(Matthew 27:3-10)

"AND the LORD sent Nathan unto David, and he came unto him, and said unto him, There were two men in one city; the one rich, and the other poor."

"The rich man had exceeding many flocks and herds:"

"But the poor man had nothing, save one little ewe lamb, which he had bought and nourished up: and it grew up together with him, and with his children; it did eat of his own meat, and drank of his own cup, and lay in his bosom, and was unto him as a daughter."

"And there came a traveller unto the rich man, and he spared to take of his own flock and of his own herd, to dress for the wayfaring man that was come unto him; but took the poor man's lamb, and dressed it for the man that was come to him."

"And David's anger was greatly kindled against the man; and he said to Nathan, As the LORD liveth, the man that hath done this thing shall surely die:"

"And he shall restore the lamb fourfold, because he did this thing, and because he had no pity."

"And Nathan said to David, Thou art the man. Thus saith the LORD God of Israel, I anointed thee king over Israel, and I delivered thee out of the hand of Saul;"

"And I gave thee thy master's house, and thy master's wives into thy bosom, and gave thee the house of Israel and of Judah; and if that had been too little, I would moreover have given thee such and such things."

"Wherefore hast thou despised the commandment of the LORD, to do evil in his sight? thou hast killed

U-ri'-ah the Hit'-tite with the sword, and hast taken his wife to be thy wife, and hast slain him with the sword of the children of Ammon."

"Now therefore the sword shall never depart from thine house; because thou hast despised me, and hast taken the wife of U-ri'-ah the Hit'-tite to be thy wife."

"Thus saith the LORD, Behold, I will raise up evil against thee out of thine own house, and I will take thy wives before thine eyes, and give them unto thy neighbour, and he shall lie with thy wives in the sight of this sun."

"For thou didst it secretly: but I will do this thing before all Israel, and before the sun."

"And David said unto Nathan, I have sinned against the LORD, And Nathan said unto David, The LORD also hath put away thy sin; thou shalt not die."

Then David confessed to Nathan, "I have sinned against the LORD."

God wants us to know that the consequences of sin always include deep regret.

(II Samuel 12:1-23)

PROMISE FROM GOD

"For godly sorrow worketh repentance to salvation not to be repented of: but the sorrow of the world worketh death."

(II Corinthians 7:10)

REJECTION

75. How can I recover from rejection in my life?

"WHO hath believed our report? and to whom is the arm of the LORD revealed?"

"For he shall grow up before him as a tender plant, and as a root out of a dry ground; he hath no form nor comeliness; and when we shall see him, there is no beauty that we should desire him."

"He is despised and rejected of men; a man of sorrows, and acquainted with grief: and we hid as it were our faces from him; he was despised, and we esteemed him not."

"Surely he hath borne our griefs, and carried our sorrows; yet we did esteem him stricken, smitten of God, and afflicted."

"But he was wounded for our transgressions, he was bruised for our iniquities: the chastisement of our peace was upon him; and with his stripes we are healed."

"All we like sheep have gone astray; we have turned every one to his own way; and the LORD hath laid on him the iniquity of us all."

"He was oppressed, and he was afflicted, yet he opened not his mouth: he is brought as a lamb to the slaughter, and as sheep before her shearers is dumb, so he openeth not his mouth."

"He was taken from prison and from judgment: and who shall declare his generation? For he was cut off out of the land of the living: for the transgression of my people was he stricken."

"And he made his grave with the wicked, and with the rich in his death; because he had done no violence, neither was any deceit in his mouth."

"Yet it pleased the LORD to bruise him; he hath put him to grief: when thou shalt make his soul an offering for sin, he shall see his seed, he shall prolong his days, and the pleasure of the LORD shall prosper in his hand."

"He shall see of the travail of his soul, and shall be satisfied: by his knowledge shall my righteous servant justify many; for he shall bear their iniquities."

"Therefore will I divide him a portion with the great, and he shall divide the spoil with the strong; because he hath poured out his soul unto death: and he was numbered with the transgressors; and he bare the sin of many, and made intercession for the transgressors."

As the prophet looks forward to the Messiah, who would be despised and rejected by others, we know we have a Savior who understands.

(Isaiah 53:1-12)

"Casting all your care upon him; for he careth for you."

Don't try to deal with rejection by yourself. Bring your concerns to God.

(I Peter 5:7)

"If ye love me, keep my commandments."

"And I will pray the Father, and he shall give you another Comforter, that he may abide with you for ever;"

"Even the Spirit of truth; whom the world cannot receive, because it seeth him not, neither knoweth him: but ye know him; for he dwelleth with you, and shall be in you."

"I will not leave you comfortless: I will come to you."

"Yet a little while, and the world seeth me no more; but ye see me: because I live, ye shall live also."

"At that day ye shall know that I am in my Father, and ye in me, and I in you."

"He that hath my commandments, and keepeth them, he it is that loveth me: and he that loveth me shall be loved of my Father, and I will love him, and will manifest myself to him."

"Judas saith unto him, not Is-car'-i-ot, Lord, how is it that thou wilt manifest thyself unto us, and not unto the world?"

"Jesus answered and said unto him, If a man love me, he will keep my words: and my Father will love him, and we will come unto him, and make our abode with him."

"He that loveth me not keepeth not my sayings: and the word which ye hear is not mine, but the Father's which sent me."

"These things have I spoken unto you, being yet present with you."

"But the Comforter, which is the Holy Ghost, whom the Father will send in my name, he shall teach you all things, and bring all things to your remembrance, whatsoever I have said unto you."

Invite the Holy Spirit into your life. Jesus promised that the Holy Spirit would stay with us forever.

(John 14:15-26)

"For I am persuaded, that neither death, nor life, nor angels, nor principalities, nor powers, nor things present, nor things to come,"

Remember that, though others may reject us, nothing can separate us from God's love.

(Romans 8:38)

76. Will God ever reject me?

"WHEN therefore the Lord knew how the Pharisees had heard that Jesus made and baptized more disciples than John,"

"(Though Jesus himself baptized not, but his disciples,)"

"He left Ju-dae'-a, and departed again into Galilee."

"And he must needs go through Sa-ma'-ri-a."

"Then cometh he to a city of Sa-ma'-ri-a, which is called Sy'-char, near to the parcel of ground that Jacob gave to his son Joseph."

"Now Jacob's well was there. Jesus therefore, being wearied with his journey, sat this on the well: and it was about the sixth hour."

"There cometh a woman of Sa-ma'-ri-a to draw water; Jesus saith unto her, Give me to drink."

"(For his disciples were gone away unto the city to buy meat.)"

"Then saith the woman of Sa-ma'-ri-a unto him, How is it that thou, being a Jew, askest drink of me, which am a woman of Sa-ma'-ri-a? For the Jews have no dealings with the Sa-mar'-i-tans."

"Jesus answered and said unto her, If thou knewest the gift of God, and who it is that saith to thee, Give me to drink; thou wouldest have asked of him, and he would have given thee living water."

"The woman saith unto him, Sir, thou hast nothing to draw with, and the well is deep:

from whence then hast thou that living water?"

"Art thou greater than our father Jacob, which gave us the well, and drank thereof himself, and his children, and his cattle?"

"Jesus answered and said unto her, Whosoever drinketh of this water shall thirst again:"

"But whosoever drinketh of the water that I shall give him shall never thirst; but the water that I shall give him shall be in him a well of water springing up into everlasting life."

"The woman saith unto him, Sir, give me this water, that I thirst not, neither come hither to draw."

"Jesus saith unto her, Go, call thy husband, and come hither."

"The woman answered and said, I have no husband. Jesus said unto her, Thou hast well said, I have no husband:"

For thou hast had five husbands; and he whom thou now hast is not thy husband: in that saidst thou truly."

"The woman saith unto him, Sir, I perceive that thou art a prophet."

"Our fathers worshipped in this mountain; and ye say, that in Jerusalem is the place where men ought to worship."

"Jesus saith unto her, Woman, believe me, the hour cometh, when ye shall neither in this mountain, nor yet at Jerusalem, worship the Father."

"Ye worship ye know not what: we know what we worship: for salvation is of the Jews."

"But the hour cometh, and now is, when the true worshippers shall worship the Father in spirit and in truth: for the Father seeketh such to worship him."

"God is a Spirit: and they that worship him must worship him in spirit and in truth."

"The woman saith unto him, I know that Mes-si'-as cometh, which is called Christ:

when he is come, he will tell us all things."

"Jesus saith unto her, I that speak unto thee am he."

Jesus did not reject the sinful Samaritan woman, but rather offered her living water.

(John 4:1-26)

"JESUS went unto the mount of Olives."

"And early om the morning he came again into the temple, and all the people came unto him; and he sat down, and taught them."

"And the scribes and Pharisees brought unto him a woman taken in adultery; and when they had set her in the midst,"

"They say unto him, Master, this woman was taken in adultery, in the very act."

"Now Moses in the law commanded us, that such should be stoned: but what sayest thou?"

"This they said, tempting him, that they might have to accuse him. But Jesus stooped down, and with his finger wrote on the ground, as though he heard them not."

"So when they continued asking him, he lifted up himself, and said unto them, He that is without sin among you, let him first cast a stone at her."

"And again he stooped down, and wrote on the ground."

"And they which heard it, being convicted by their own conscience, went out one by one, beginning at the eldest, even unto the last: and Jesus was left alone, and the woman standing in the midst."

"When Jesus had lifted up himself, and saw none but the woman, he said unto her, Woman, where are those thine accusers? Hath no man comdemned thee?"

"She said, No man, Lord. And Jesus said unto her, Neither do I condemn thee: go, And sin no more."

Jesus rejects the sin without rejecting the sinner.

(John 8:1-11)

"All that the Father giveth me shall come to me; and him that cometh to me I will in no wise cast out."

The Lord Jesus accepts all who come to him in faith.

(John 6:37)

PROMISE FROM GOD

"Let your conversation be without covetousness; and be content with such things as ye have: for he hath said, I WILL NEVER LEAVE THEE, NOR FORSAKE THEE."

(Hebrews 13:5)

REPENTANCE

77. Why is repentance necessary?

"Therefore, O thou son of man, speak unto the house of Israel; Thus ye speak, saying, If our transgressions and our sins be upon us, and we pine away in them, how should we then live?"

"Say unto them, As I live, saith the Lord GOD, I have no pleasure in the death of the wicked; but that the wicked turn from his way and live: turn ye, turn ye from your evil ways; for why will ye die, O house of Israel?"

"Therefore, thou son of man, say unto the children of thy people, The righteousness of the righteous shall not deliver him in the day of his transgression: as for the wickedness of the wicked, he shall turneth from his wickedness; neither shall the righteous be able to live for his righteousness in the day that he sinneth."

"When I shall say to the righteous, that he shall surely live; if he trust to his own righteousness, and commit iniquity, all his righteousness shall not be remembered; but for his iniquity that he hath committed, he shall die for it."

"Again, when I say unto the wicked, Thou shalt surely die; if he turn from his sin, and do that which is lawful and right;"

"If the wicked restore the pledge, give again that he had robbed, walk in the statutes of life, without committing iniquity; he shall surely live, he shall not die."

"None of his sins that he hath committed shall be mentioned unto him: he hath done that which is lawful and right; he shall surely live."

Repentance leads to forgiveness of sin.

(Ezekiel 33:10-16)

O LORD, are not thine eyes upon the truth? Thou hast stricken them, but they have not grieved; thou hast consumed them, but they have refused to receive correction: they have made their faces harder than a rock; they have refused to return."

They are determined, with faces set like stone, they have refused to repent.

The unrepentant heart rejects God and remains in sin's grasp.

(Jeremiah 5:3)

"THERE were present at that season some that told him of the Gal-i-lae'-ans, whose blood Pilate had mingled with their sacrifices."

"And Jesus answering said unto them, Suppose ye that these Gal-i-lae'-ans, because they suffered such things?"

"I tell you, Nay: but, except ye repent, ye shall all likewise perish."

"Or those eighteen, upon whom the tower in Si-lo'-am fell, and slew them, think ye that they were sinners above all men that dwelt in Jerusalem?"

"I tell you, Nay: but, except ye repent, ye shall all likewise perish."

"He spake also this parable; A certain man had a fig tree planted in his vineyard; and he came and sought fruit thereon, and found none."

"Then said he unto the dresser of his vineyard, Behold, these three years I come seeking fruit on this fig tree, and find none: cut it down; why cumbereth it the ground?"

"And he answering said unto him, Lord, let it alone this year also, till I shall dig about it, and dung it:"

Jesus taught that without repentance we face judgment.

(Luke 13:1-8)

"Likewise, I say unto you, there is joy in the presence of the angels of God over one sinner that repenteth."

All heaven rejoices when one sinner repents.

(Luke 15:10)

78. What is repentance?

"IN those days came John the Baptist, preaching in the wilderness of Ju-dae'-a."

"And saying, Repent ye: for the kingdom of heaven is at hand."

"For this is he that was spoken of by the prophet E-sa'-ias, saying, THE VOICE OF ONE CRYING IN THE WILDERNESS, PREPARE YE THE WAY OF THE LORD, MAKE HIS PATHS STRAIGHT."

Repentance means being sorry for sin and being committed to a new way of life, serving God.

(Matthew 3:1-3)

"And Zac-chae'-us stood, and said unto the Lord; Behold, Lord, the half of my goods I give to the poor; and if I have taken any thing from any man by false accusation, I restore him fourfold."

Repentance is made complete by changed behavior.

(Luke 19:8)

"And Pharaoh sent, and called for Moses and Aaron, and said unto them, I have sinned this time: the LORD is righteous, and I and my people are wicked."

"Intreat the LORD (for it is enough) that there be no more mighty thunderings and hail;

and I will let you go, and ye shall stay no longer."

And Moses said unto him, As soon as I am gone out of the city, I will spread abroad my hands unto the LORD; and the thunder shall cease, neither shall there be any more hail;

that thou mayest know how that the earth is the LORD's."

"But as for thee and thy servants, I know that ye will not yet fear the LORD God."

"And the flax and the barley was smitten: for the barley was in the ear, and the flax was boiled."

"But the wheat and the rie were not smitten: for they were not grown up."

"And Moses went out of the city from Pharaoh, and spread abroad his hands unto the LORD: and the thunder and hail ceased, and the rain was not poured upon the earth."

"And when Pharaoh saw that the rain and the hail and the thunders were ceased, he sinned yet more, and hardened his heart, he and his servants."

And the heart of Pharaoh was hardened, neither would he let the children of Israel go; as the LORD had spoken by Moses."

Repentance that produces no lasting change is insincere.

(Exodus 9:27-35)

79. Is repentance a one-time event, or do we need to repent each time we sin?

"For thou desirest not sacrifice; else would I give it: thou delightest not in burnt offering."

"The sacrifices of God are a broken spirit: a broken and a contrite heart, O God, thou wilt not despise."

While salvation is a one time occasion, God is pleased by a broken and repentant heart ready to confess and repent of sin.

(Psalm 51:16, 17)

"If we say that we have no sin, we deceive ourselves, and the truth is not in us."

"If we confess our sins, he is faithful and just to forgive us our sins, and cleanse us from all righteousness."

Confession and repentance of sin are a constant mark of the person walking in the light of fellowship with God.

(I John 1:8, 9)

PROMISE FROM GOD

"Then Peter said unto them, Repent, and be baptized every one of you in the name of Jesus Christ for the remission of sins, and ye shall receive the gift of the Holy Ghost.

(Acts 2:38)

REPUTATION

80. Should Christians be concerned about their reputation?

"And we have sent with him the brother, whose praise is in the gospel throughout all the churches;"

"And not that only, but who was also chosen of the churches to travel with us with this grace, which is administered by us to the glory of the same Lord, and declaration of your ready mind:"

"Avoiding this, that no man should blame us in this abundance which administered by us:"

"Providing for honest things, not only in the sight of the Lord, but also in the sight of men."

"And we have sent with them our brother, whom we have oftentimes proved diligent in many things, but now much more diligent, upon the great confidence which I have in you."

"Whether any do enquire of Titus, he is my partner and fellowhelper concerning you: or our brethren be enquired of, they are the messengers of the churches, and the glory of Christ."

"Wherefore shew ye to them, and before the churches, the proof of your love, and of our boasting on your behalf."

We should take care to construct a reputation of uprightness so the ministry of the gospel isn't hindered.

(II Corinthians 8:18-24)

"TAKE heed that ye do not your alms before men, to be seen of them: otherwise ye have no reward of your Father which is in heaven."

"Therefore when thou doest thine alms, do not sound a trumpet before thee, as the hypocrites do in the synagogues and in the streets, that they may have glory of men.

Verily I say unto you, They have their reward."

"But when thou doest alms, let not thy left hand know what thy right hand doeth:"

"That thine alms may be in secret: and thy Father which seeth in secret himself shall reward thee openly."

"And when thou prayest, thou shalt not be as the hypocrites are: for they love to pray standing in the synagogues and in the street corners of the streets, that they may be seen of men. Verily I say unto you, They have their reward."

"But thou, when thou prayest, enter into thy closet, and when thou hast shut thy door, pray to thy Father which is in secret; and thy Father which seeth in secret shall reward thee openly."

"But when ye pray, use not vain repetitions, as the heathen do: for they think that they shall be heard for their much speaking."

"Be not ye therefore like unto them: for your Father knoweth what things ye have need of, before ye ask him."

"After this manner therefore pray ye: Our Father which art in heaven, Hallowed be thy name."

"Thy kingdom come. Thy will be done in earth, as it is in heaven."

"Give us this day our daily bread."

"And forgive us our debts, as we forgive our debtors."

"And lead us not into temptation, but deliver us from evil: For thine is the kingdom, and the power, and the glory for ever. A-men'."

"For if ye forgive men their trespasses, your heavenly Father will also forgive you:"

"But if ye forgive not men their trespasses, neither will your Father forgive your trespasses."

"Moreover when ye fast, be not, as the hypocrites, of a sad countenance: for they disfigure their faces, that they may appear unto men to fast. Verily I say unto you, they have their reward."

"But thou, when thou fastest, anoint thine head, and wash thy face;"

"That thou appear not unto men to fast, but unto thy Father which is in secret: and thy Father, which seeth in secret, shall reward the openly."

Don't do your good deeds publicly, to be admired.

Jesus cautions us not to seek after spirituality so as to impress others.

(Matthew 6:1-18)

"And beside this, giving all diligence, add to your faith virtue; and to virtue knowledge;"

"And to knowledge temperance; and to temperance patience; and to patience godliness;"

"And to godliness brotherly kindness; and to brotherly kindness charity."

"For if these things be in you, and abound, they make you that ye shall neither be barren nor unfruitful in the knowledge of our Lord Jesus Christ."

"But he that lacketh these things is blind, and cannot see afar off, and hath forgotten that he was purged from his old sins."

Then your faith will produce a life of moral excellence.

A reputation we strive to achieve should come about because of being completely committed to building spiritual character in our life.

(II Peter 1:5-9)

81. How can a bad reputation be changed?

"Dearly beloved, I beseech you as strangers and pilgrims, abstain from fleshly lusts, which war against the soul;"

"Having your conversation honest among the Gentiles: that, whereas they speak against you as evildoers, they may by your good works, which they shall behold, glorify God in the day of visitation."

They will see your honorable behavior, and they will believe and give honor to God.

The surest way to influence the manner in which others think of you is by your good behavior.

(I Peter 2:11, 12)

"Behold, I have taught you statutes and judgments, even as the LORD my God commanded me, that ye should do so in the land whither ye go to possess it."

"Keep therefore and do them; for this is your wisdom and your understanding in the sight of the nations, which shall hear all these statues, and say, Surely this great nation is a wise and understanding people."

"For what nation is there so great, who hath God so nigh unto them, as the LORD our God is in all things that we call upon him for?"

"And what nation is there so great, that hath statutes and judgments so righteous as all this law, which I set before you this day?"

If you obey them carefully, you will display your wisdom and intelligence to the surrounding nations.

Obedience to God brings a reputation for wisdom and intelligence.

(Deuteronomy 4:5-8)

"And it came to pass, that, as Jesus sat at meat in his house, many publicans and sinners sat also together with Jesus and his disciples: for there were many, and they followed him."

"And when the scribes and Pharisees saw him eat with publicans and sinners, they said unto his disciples, How is it that he eatheth and drinketh with publicans and sinners?"

"When Jesus heard it, he saith unto them. They that are whole have no need of the physician, but they that are sick: I came not to call the righteous, but sinners to repentance."

Jesus doesn't accept us based on our reputation, but because his love transform sinners.

(Mark 2:15-17)

"For I rejoiced greatly, when the brethren came and testified of the truth that is in thee, even as thou walkest in the truth."

"I have no greater joy than to hear that my children walk in truth."

"Beloved, thou doest faithfully whatsoever thou doest to the brethren, and to strangers;"

"Which have borne witness of thy charity before the church: whom if thou bring forward on their journey after a godly sort, thou shalt do well;"

May we earn the reputation of living according to the standards of the gospel for purity and truth.

(III John 1:3-6)

PROMISE FROM GOD

"Humble yourselves therefore under the mighty hand of God, that he may exalt you in due time:"

So humble yourselves under the mighty power of God, and in his good time he will honor you.

(I Peter 5:6)

RESPECT

82. How do I gain respect?

"But ye, beloved, building up yourselves on your most holy faith, praying in the Holy Ghost."

But you, dear friends, must continue to build your lives on the foundation of your holy faith.

(Jude 1:20)

"Therefore all things whatsoever ye would that men should do to you, do ye even so to them: for this is the law and the prophets."

Do for others what you would like them to do for you.

(Matthew 7:12)

"But glory, honour, and peace, to every man that worketh good, to the Jew first, and also to the Gentile:"

We gain respect similarly (the same way) that we show it-building our lives on God's Word, treating others the way in which we may want to be treated, not compromising our character, and standing up for truth no matter what.

(Romans 2:10)

83. How do we show respect to others?

"And Jesus answering said, A certain man went down from Jerusalem to Jericho, and fell among thieves, which stripped him of his raiment, and wounded him, and departed, leaving him half dead."

"And by chance there came down a certain priest that way: and when he saw him, he passed by on the other side."

"And likewise a Levite, when he was at the place, came and looked on him, and passed by on the other side."

"But a certain Sa-mar'-i-tan, as he journeyed, came where he was: and when he saw him, he had compassion on him."

"And went to him, and bound up his wounds, pouring in oil and wine, and set him on his own beast, and brought him to an inn, and took care of him."

"And on the morrow when he departed, he took out two pence, and gave them to the host, and said unto him, Take care of him; and whatsoever thou spendest more, when I come again, I will repay thee."

"Which now of these three, thinkest thou, was neighbour unto him that fell among the thieves?

"And he said, He that shewed mercy on him. Then said Jesus unto him, Go, and do thou likewise."

(Luke 10:30-37)

"Be kindly affectioned one to another with brotherly love; in honour preferring one another."

(Romans 12:10)

"Let nothing be done through strife or vainglory; but in lowliness of mind let each esteem other better than themselves."

Be humble, thinking of others as better than yourself.

(Philippians 2:3)

"Honour all men, Love the brotherhood. Fear God. Honour the king."

Love your Christian brothers and sisters. And Fear God.

(I Peter 2:17)

"And we beseech you, brethren, to know them which labour among you, and are over you in the Lord, and admonish you:"

Honour those who are your leaders in the Lord's work.

(I Thessalonians 5:12)

"Render therefore to all their dues: tribute to whom tribute is due; custom to whom custom; fear to whom fear; honour to whom honour."

Give to everyone what you owe them.

(Romans 13:7)

"NOW as touching things offered unto idols, we know that we all have knowledge, Knowledge puffeth up, but charity edifieth."

It is love that really builds up the church.

(I Corinthians 8:1)

"MY brethren, have not the faith of our Lord Jesus Christ, the Lord of glory, with respect of persons."

How can you claim that you have faith in our glorious Lord Jesus Christ if you favor some people more than others?

Respect involves showing more concern for people than plans or agendas, having a favorable opinion of others, building them up in love, and treating everybody with fairness and integrity.

(James 2:1)

84. Whom should we honor and respect?

"O LORD, I beseech thee, let now thine ear be attentive to the prayer of thy servant, and to the prayer of thy servants, who desire to fear thy name: and prosper, I pray thee, thy servant this day, and grant him mercy in the sight of this man. For I was the king's cupbearer."

Listen to the prayers of those of us who take pleasure in honoring you.

(Nehemiah 1:11)

"Thou art worthy, O Lord, to receive glory and honour and power: for thou hast created all things, and for thy pleasure they are and were created."

God, to receive glory and honor and power. For you created everything.

(Revelation 4:11)

"Honour thy father and thy mother; that thy days may be long upon the land which the LORD thy God giveth thee."

(Exodus 20:12)

"Thou shalt rise up before the hoary head, and honour the face of the old man, and fear thy God: I am the LORD."

(Leviticus 19:32)

"And it came to pass afterward, that David's heart smote him, because he had cut off Saul's skirt."

"And he said unto his men, The LORD forbid that I should do this thing unto my master, the LORD's anointed, to stretch forth mine hand against him, seeing he is the anointed of the LORD."

"So David stayed his servants with these words, and suffered them not to rise against Saul. But Saul rose up out of the cave, and went on his way.

It is a serious thing to attack the LORD's anointed one.

Those in authority over us.

(I Samuel 24:5-7)

"Be kindly affectioned one to another with brotherly love; in honour preferring one another."

Love each other with genuine affection, and take delight in honoring each other.

(Romans 12:10)

PROMISE FROM GOD

"For whosoever exalteth himself shall be abased; and he that humbleth himself shall be exalted."

For the proud will be humbled, but the humble will be honored.

(Luke 14:11)

RESPONSIBILITY

85. What does the Bible say about personal responsibility?

"And the man said, The woman whom thou gavest to be with me, she gave me of the tree, and I did eat."

"And the LORD God said unto the woman, What is this that thou hast done? And the woman said, The serpent beguiled me, and I did eat."

When confronted by God for his sin Adam blamed someone else.

(Genesis 3:12, 13)

"Now at that feast the governor was wont to release unto the people a prisoner, whom they would."

"And they had then a notable prisoner, called Bar-ab'-ras."

"Therefore when they were gathered together, Pilate said unto them, Whom will ye that I release unto you? Bar-ab'-has, or Jesus which is called Christ?"

"For he knew that for envy they had delivered him."

"When he was set down on the judgment seat, his wife sent unto him, saying, Have thou nothing to do with that just man: for I have suffered many things this day in a dream because of him."

"But the chief priests and elders persuaded the multitude that they should ask Bar-ab'-bas, and destory Jesus."

"The governor answered and said unto them, Whether of the twain will ye that I release unto you? They said, Bar-ab'-bas."

"Pilate saith unto them, What shall I do then with Jesus which is called Christ? They all say unto him, Let him be crucified."

"And the governor said, Why, what evil hath he done? But they cried out the more, saying, Let him be crucified."

"When Pilate saw that he could prevail nothing, but that rather a tumult was made, he took water, and washed his hands before the multitude, saying, I am innocent of the blood of this just person: see ye to it."

"Then answered all the people, and said, His blood be on us, and on our children."

"Then released he Bar-ab'-bas unto them: and when he had scourged Jesus, he delivered him to be crucified."

In attempting to avoid his own responsibility, Pilate sent Jesus to the cross.

(Matthew 27:15-26)

"But thou shalt appoint the Levites over the tabernacle of testimony, and over all the vessels thereof, and over all things that belong to it: they shall bear the tabernacle, and all the vessels thereof; and they shall minister unto it, and shall encamp round about the tabernacle."

"And when the tabernacle setteth forward, the Levites shall take it down: and when the tabernacle is to be pitched, the Levites shall set it up; and the stranger that cometh nigh shall be put to death."

A portion of our duties may appear to be boring or dull, however, it is important to God that we fulfill them wholeheartedly.

(Numbers 1:50, 51)

"Be not deceived; God is not mocked: for whatsoever a man soweth, that shall he also reap."

"For he that soweth to his flesh shall of the flesh reap corruption; but he that soweth to the Spirit shall of the Spirit reap life everlasting."

We can not ignore God and get away with it.

We are each liable for our own conduct (behavior) and will bear the consequences-now and in eternity.

(Galatians 6:7, 8)

86. What are my responsibilities before God?

"Having then gifts differing according to the grace that is given to us, whether prophecy, let us prophesy according to the proportion of faith;"

"Or ministry, let us wait on our ministering: or he that teacheth, on teaching;"

"Or he that exhorteth, on exhortation: he that giveth, let him do it with simplicity; he that ruleth, with diligence; he that shewth mercy, with cheerfulness."

We are responsible to use the gifts God has given for the good of the church.

(Romans 12:6-8)

"Beloved, let us love one another: for love is of God; and every one that loveth is born of God, and knoweth God."

"He that loveth not knoweth not God; for God is love."

"In this was manifested the love of God toward us, because that God sent his only begotten Son into the world, that we might live through him."

"Herein is love, not that we loved God, but that he loved us, and sent his Son to be the propitiation for our sins."

"Beloved, if God so loved us, we ought also to love one another."

"No man hath seen God at any time. If we love one another, God dwelleth in us, and his love is perfected in us."

"Hereby know we that we dwell in him, and he in us, because he hath given us of his Spirit."

"And we have seen and do testify that the Father sent the Son to be Saviour of the world."

"Whosoever shall confess that Jesus is the Son of God, God dwelleth in him, and he in God."

"And we have known and believed the love that God hath to us. God is love; and he that dwelleth in love dwelleth in God, and God in him."

"Herein is our love made perfect, that we may have boldness in the day of judgment:

because as he is, so are we in this world."

Our greatest responsibility is to love God by loving others.

(I John 4:7-17)

PROMISE FROM GOD

"For unto every one that hath shall be given, and he shall have abundance: but from him that hath not shall be taken away from even that which he hath."

(Matthew 25:29)

REST

87. Who can afford to take time to rest with so much to do?

"THUS the heavens and the earth were finished, and all the host of them."

"And on the seventh day God ended his work which he had made; and he rested on the seventh day from all his work he had made."

"And God blessed the seventh day, and sanctified it: because that in it he had rested from all his work which God created and made."

If God saw rest from work as holy, how can we afford not to rest?

(Genesis 2:1-3)

"Remember the sabbath day, to keep it holy."

"Six days shalt thou labour, and do all thy work:"

"But the seventh day is the sabbath of the LORD thy God: in it thou shalt not do any work, thou, nor thy son, nor thy daughter, they manservant, nor thy maidservant, nor thy cattle, nor thy stranger that is within thy gates:"

"For in six days the LORD made heaven and earth, the sea, and all that in them is, and rested the seventh day: wherefore the LORD blessed the sabbath day, and hallowed it."

The seventh day is a day of rest dedicated to the LORD your God.

(Exodus 20:8-11)

88. How can I experience the refreshment God promises?

"THE LORD is my shepherd; I shall not want."

"He maketh me to lie down in green pastures: he leadeth me beside the still waters.

"He restoreth my soul: he leadeth me in the paths of righteousness for his name's sake."

As we follow Jesus ever more closely, we will experience the rest and refreshment of his presence.

(Psalm 23:1-3)

"Come unto me, all ye that labour and are heavy laden, and I will give you rest."

"Take my yoke upon you, and learn of me; for I am meek and lowly in heart: and ye shall find rest unto your souls."

"For my yoke is easy, and my burden is light."

The final and ultimate rest is the promise of heaven for those who put their faith in Christ.

(Matthew 11:28-30)

"LET us therefore fear, lest, a promise being left us of entering into his rest, any of you should seem to come short of it."

"For unto us was the gospel preached, as well as unto them: but the word preached did not profit them, not being mixed with faith in them that heard it."

"For we which have believed do enter into rest, as he said, AS I HAVE SWORN IN MY WRATH, IF THEY SHALL ENTER INTO MY REST: although the works were finished from the foundation of the world."

"For he spake in a certain place of the seventh day on this wise, AND GOD DID REST THE SEVENTH DAY FROM ALL HIS WORKS."

"And in this place again, IF THEY SHALL ENTER INTO MY REST."

"Seeing therefore it remaineth that some must enter therein, and they to whom it was first preached entered not in because of unbelief:"

"Again, he limiteth a certain day, saying in David, TO DAY IF YE WILL HEAR HIS VOICE, HARDEN NOT YOUR HEARTS."

"For if Jesus had given them rest, then would he not afterward have spoken of another day."

"There remaineth therefore a rest to the people of God."

"For he that is entered into his rest, he also hath ceased from his own works, as God did from his."

"Let us labour therefore to enter into that rest, lest any man fall after the same example of unbelief."

The final and ultimate rest is the promise of heaven for those who put their faith in Christ.

(Hebrews 4:1-11)

PROMISE FROM GOD

"He giveth power to the faint; and to them that have no might he increaseth strength."

"Even the youths shall faint and be weary, and the young men shall utterly fall:

"But they that wait upon the LORD shall renew their strength; they shall mount up with wings as eagles; they shall run, and not be weary; and they shall walk, and not faint."

(Isaiah 40:29-31)

RESTLESSNESS

89. Is restlessness bad?

"THEN came the children of Israel, even the whole congregation, into the desert of Zin in the first month: and the people abode in Ka'-desh; and Miriam died there, and was buried there.

"And there was no water for the congregation: and they gathered themselves together against Moses and against Aaron."

"And the people chode with Moses, and spake, saying, Would God that we had died when our brethren died before the LORD!"

"And why have ye brought up the congregation of the LORD into this wilderness, that we and our cattle should die there?"

"And wherefore have ye made us to come up out of Egypt, to bring us in unto this evil place? It is no place of seed, or of figs, or of vines, or of pomegranates; neither is there any water to drink."

"And Moses and Aaron went from the presence of the assembly unto the door of the tabernacle of the congregation, and they fell upon their faces: and the glory of the LORD appeared unto them."

"And the LORD spake unto Moses, saying,"

"Take the rod, and gather thou the assembly together, thou, and Aaron thy brother, and speak ye unto the rock before their eyes; and it shall five forth his water, and thou shalt bring forth to them water out of the rock: so thou shalt give the congregation and their beasts drink."

"And Moses took the rod from before the LORD, as he commanded him."

"And Moses and Aaron gathered the congregation together before the rock, and he said unto them, Hear now, ye rebels; must we fetch you water out of this rock?"

"And Moses lifted up his hand, and with his rod he smote the rock twice: and the water came out abundantly, and the congregation drank and their beasts also."

"And the LORD spake unto Moses and Aaron, Because ye believed me not, to sanctify me in the eyes of the children of Israel, therefore ye shall not bring this congregation into the land which I have given them."

"This is the water of Mer'-i-bah; because the children of Israel strove with the LORD, and he was sanctified in them."

Restlessness rooted in selfish impatience can lead us into sin.

(Numbers 20:1-13)

"I the Preacher was king over Israel in Jerusalem."

"Let us hear the conclusion of the whole matter; Fear God, and keep his commandments: for this is the whole duty of man."

"For God shall bring every work into judgment, with every secret thing, whether it be good, or whether it be evil."

A restless search for truth can lead to a deeper understanding of God and his purposes.

(Ecclesiastes 1:12; 12:13, 14)

90. How do I find peace?

"Come unto me, all ye that labour and ae heavy laden, and I will give you rest."

"Take my yoke upon you, and learn of me; for I am meek and lowly in heart: and ye shall find rest unto your souls."

"For my yoke is easy, and my burden is light."

Jesus promises his peace to all who come to him in trusting faith.

(Matthew 11:28-30)

"THEREFORE being justified by faith, we have peace with God through our Lord Jesus Christ."

"By whom also we have access by faith into this grace wherein we stand, and rejoice in hope of the glory of God."

Jesus promises his peace to all who come to him in trusting faith.

(Romans 5:1, 2)

PROMISE FROM GOD

"Be careful for nothing; but in every thing by prayer and supplication with thanksgiving let your requests be made known unto God."

"And the peace of God, which passeth all understanding, shall keep your hearts and minds through Christ Jesus."

(Philippians 4:6, 7)

REVENGE

91. Is revenge ever justified?

"Thou shalt not hate thy brother in thine heart: thou shalt in any wise rebuke thy neighbour, and not suffer sin upon him."

Taking personal revenge is expressly forbidden by God.

(Leviticus 19:18)

"THE burden of Nin'-e-veh. The book of the vision of Na'-hum the El'-kosh-ite."

"God is jealous, and the LORD revengeth; the LORD revengeth, and is furious; the LORD will take vengeance on his adversaries, and he reserveth wrath for his enemies."

"The LORD is slow to anger, and great in power, and will not at all acquit the wicked: the LORD hath his way in the whirlwind and in the storm, and the clouds are the dust of his feet."

"He rebuketh the sea, and maketh it dry, and drieth up all the rivers: Ba'-shan languisheth, and Carmel, and the flower of Leb'-a-non languisheth."

""The mountains quake at him, and the hills melt, and the earth is burned at his presence, yea, the world, and all that dwell therein."

"Who can stand before his indignation? and who can abide in the fierceness of his anger? his fury is poured out like fire, and rocks are thrown down by him."

"The LORD is good, a strong hold in the day of trouble; and he knoweth them that trust in him."

"But with an overrunning flood he will make an utter end of the place thereof, and darkness shall pursue his enemies."

God's vengeance isn't to get back or settle the score (get even), but to administer righteous judgment.

(Nahum 1:1-8)

"Thou hast heard my voice: hide not thine ear at my breathing, at my cry."

"Thou drewest near in the day that I called upon thee: thou saidst Fear not."

"O Lord, thou hast pleaded the causes of my soul; thou hast redeemed my life."

"O LORD, thou hast seen my wrong; judge thou my cause."

"Thou hast seen all their vengeance and all their imaginations against me."

"Thou hast heard their reproach, O LORD, and all their imaginations against me;"

"The lips of those that rose up against me, and their device against me all the day."

"Behold their sitting down, and their rising up; I am their musick."

"Render unto them a recompence, O LORD, according to the work of their hands."

"Give them sorrow of heart, thy curse unto them."

"Persecute and destroy them in anger from under the heavens of the LORD."

You have seen the wrong they have done to me, LORD. Be my judge, and prove me right.

(Lamentations 3:55-66)

"Which is a manifest token of the righteous judgment of God, that ye may be counted worthy of the kingdom of God, for which ye also suffer:"

"Seeing it is a righteous thing with God to recompense tribulation to them that trouble you;"

"And to you who are troubled rest with us, when the Lord Jesus shall be revealed from heaven with his mighty angels,"

"In flaming fire taking vengeance on them that know not God, and that obey not the gospel of our Lord Jesus Christ:"

"Who shall be punished with everlasting destruction from the presence of the Lord, and from the glory of his power;"

"When he shall come to be glorified in his saints, and to be admired in all them that believe (because our testimony among you was believed) in that day."

We don't have to take vengeance into our own hands, for God will judge and punish all wickedness.

(II Thessalonians 1:5-10)

"Recompense to no man evil for evil. Provide things honest in the sight of all men."

"If it be possible, as much as lieth in you, live peaceably with all men."

"Dearly beloved, avenge not yourselves, but rahter give place unto wrath: for it is written, VENGEANCE IS MINE; I WILL REPAY, saith the Lord."

"Therefore IF THINE ENEMY HUNGER, FEED HIM; IF HE THIRST, GIVE HIM DRINK: FOR IN SO DOING THOU SHALT HEAP COALS OF FIRE ON HIS HEAD."

"Be not overcome of evil, but overcome evil with good."

One wrongdoing never justifies a second.

(Romans 12:17-21)

"For even hereunto were ye called: because Christ also suffered for us, leaving us an example, that ye should follow his steps:"

"WHO DID NO SIN, NEITHER WAS GUILE FOUND IN HIS MOUTH:"

"Who, when he was reviled, reviled not again; when he suffered, he threatened not; but committed himself to him that judgeth righteously:"

"Who his own self bare our sins in his own body on the tree, that we, being dead to sins, should live unto righteousness: BY WHOSE STRIPES YE WERE HEALED."

"FOR YE WERE AS SHEEP GOING ASTRAY; BUT ARE NOW RETURNED UNTO the Shepherd and Bishop of your souls."

Jesus is our example of refusing to take revenge against those who mistreat us.

(I Peter 2:21-25)

PROMISE FROM GOD

"Whoso diggeth a pit shall fall therein: and he that rolleth a stone, it will return upon him."

(Proverbs 26:27)

SAFETY

92. Does God protect those who love him from physical harm?

"My God hath sent his angel, and hath shut the lions' mouths, that they have not hurt me: forasmuch as before him innocency was found in me; and also before thee, O king, have I done no hurt."

"Then was the king exceeding glad for him, and commanded that they should take Daniel up out of the den. So Daniel was taken up out of the den, and no manner of hurt was found upon him, because he believed in his God."

Sometimes God protects and delivers in supernatural ways (miraculous ways) so as to safeguard us so we can keep on serving him.

(Daniel 6:22, 23)

"And lest I should be exalted above measure through the abundance of the revelations, there was given me a thorn in the flesh, the messenger of Satan to buffet me, lest I should be exalted above measure."

At other times even God's chosen servants experience devastating physical hardship and suffering. These are the times when our faith is scrutinized (put to the test), and we should not lose our eternal perspective.

(II Corinthians 12:7)

"And not only so, but we glory in tribulations also: knowing that tribulation worketh patience;"

"And patience, experience; and experience, hope:"

"And hope maketh not ashamed; because the love of God is shed abroad in our hearts by the Holy Ghost which is given unto us."

When God doesn't forestall sufferings, he promises strength to endure through the Holy Spirit.

(Romans 5:3-5)

"That thou mayest love the LORD thy God, and that thou mayest obey his voice, and that thou mayest cleave unto him: for he is thy life, and the length of thy days: that thou mayest dwell in the land which the LORD sware unto thy fathers, to Abraham, to Isaac, and to Jacob, to give them."

Choose to love the LORD your God and to obey him...Then you will live long in the land.

Through his Word, God offers wisdom that helps us avoid needless peril.

(Deuteronomy 30:20)

93. If an accident, tragedy, or illness occurs, does it mean God is punishing me for something?

"AND as Jesus passed by, he saw a man which was blind from his birth."

"And his disciples asked him, saying, Master, who did sin, this man, or his parents, that he was born blind?"

"Jesus answered, Neither hath this man sinned, nor his parents: but that the works of God should be made manifest in him."

"I must work the works of him that sent me, while it is day: the night cometh, when no man can work."

"As long as I am in the world, I am the light of the world."

God is better understood not as the cause of our suffering but as the redeemer of our sufferings.

(John 9:1-5)

94. If God doesn't guarantee physical safety, what's the point of faith?

"And now come I to thee; and these things I speak in the world, that they might have my joy fulfilled in themselves."

"I have given them thy word; and the world hath hated them, because they are not of the world, even as I am not of the world."

"I pray not that thou shouldest take them out of the world, but that thou shouldest keep them from the evil."

"They are not of the world, even as I am not of the world."

"Sanctify them through thy truth: thy word is truth."

"As thou hast sent me into the world, even so have I sent them into the world."

Faith has more to do with the eternal well-being (safety) of our souls than the physical safety of our bodies.

(John 17:13-18)

"For the which cause I also suffer these things: nevertheless I am not ashamed: for I know whom I have believed, and am persuaded that he is able to keep that which I have committed unto him against that day."

For I know the one in whom I trust, and I am sure that he is able to guard what I have entrusted to him until the day of his return.

Faith is confiding in God to guard and keep that which is eternal-our souls.

(II Timothy 1:12)

"FOR YE WERE AS SHEEP GOING ASTRAY; but are now returned unto the Shepherd and Bishop of your souls."

Christ, the Shepherd of our souls, guards us from the enemy's attacks.

(I Peter 2:25)

"For Christ also hath once suffered for sins, the just for the unjust, that he might bring us to God, being put to death in the flesh, but quickened by the Spirit:"

Faith in Jesus Christ gives us safe passage to our eternal home.

(I Peter 3:18)

95. Is it wrong, then, to pray for safety for ourselves and our loved ones?

"Peter therefore was kept in prison: but prayer was made without ceasing of the church unto God for him."

God consistently, always welcome the confession of our desires when offered in submission to his will.

(Acts 12:5)

"Making request, if by any means now at length I might have a prosperous journey by the will of God to come unto you."

Paul's desire for safety in travel was rooted in his desire to minister to others.

(Romans 1:10)

"Ye also helping together by prayer for us, that for the gift bestowed upon us by the means of many persons thanks may be given by many on our behalf."

The early apostles depended upon the prayers for safety offered by the churches.

(II Corinthians 1:11)

PROMISE FROM GOD

"The angel of the LORD encampeth round about them that fear him, and delivereth them.

For the angel of the Lord guards all who fear him, and he rescues them.

(Psalm 34:7)

SALVATION

96. What does it mean to be saved?

"Now to him that worketh is he reward not reckoned of grace, but of debt."

"But to him that worketh not, but believeth on him that justified the ungodly, his faith is counted for righteousness."

"Even as David also describeth the blessedness of the man, unto whom God imputeth righteousness without works."

What joy for those whose sin is no longer counted against them by the Lord.

(Romans 4:4-6)

"Being justified freely by his grace through the redemption that is in Christ Jesus:"

Being saved means no longer having our sins count against us but rather being forgiven by the grace of God.

(Romans 3:24)

"For as the heaven is high above the earth, so great is his mercy toward them that fear him."

"As far as the east is from the west, so far hath he removed our transgressions from us."

Being saved means our sins have been completely removed.

(Psalm 103:11, 12)

"HAVE mercy upon me, O God, according unto the multitude of thy tender mercies blot out my transgressions."

"Wash me throughly from mine iniquity, and cleanse me from my sin."

"For I acknowledge my transgressions: and my sin is ever before me."

"Against thee, thee only, have I sinned, and done this evil in thy sight: that thou mightiest be justified when thou speakest, and be clear when thou judgest."

"Behold, I was shapen in iniquity; and in sin did my mother conceive me."

"Behold, thou desirest truth in the inward parts: and in the hidden part thou shalt make me to know wisdom."

"Purge me with hyssop, and I shall be clean: wash me, and I shall be whiter than snow."

"Make me to hear joy and gladness; that the bones which thou hast broken may rejoice."

"Hide my face from my sins, and blot out all mine iniquities."

"Create in me a clean heart, O God; and renew a right spirit within me."

"Cast me not away from thy presence; and take not thy holy spirit from me."

"Restore unto me the joy of thy salvation; and uphold me with thy free spirit."

Being saved means that the stain of guilt has been washed away.

(Psalm 51:1-12)

"The Lord knoweth how to deliver the godly out of temptations, and to reserve the unjust unto the day of judgment to be punished:"

"But chiefly them that walk after the flesh in the lust of uncleanness, and despise government. Presumptuous are they, selfwilled, they are not afraid to speak evil of dignities."

Once you received none of God's mercy; now you have received his mercy.

(I Peter 2:9-10)

97. How can I be saved?

"FOR WHOSOEVER SHALL CALL UPON THE NAME OF THE LORD SHALL BE SAVED."

Anyone who calls on the name of the Lord will be saved.

(Romans 10:13)

"For God so loved the world, that he gave his only begotten Son, that whosoever believeth in him should not perish, but have everlasting life."

(John 3:16)

"Verily, verily, I say unto you, He that heareth my word, and believeth on him that sent me, hath everlasting life, and shall not come into condemnation; but is passed from death unto life."

I assure you, those who listen to my message and believe in God who sent me have eternal life.

Jesus himself promised that those who believe in him will be saved.

(John 5:24)

98. Is salvation available to anyone?

"For unto you is born this day in the city of David a Saviour, which is Christ the Lord."

"And this ahll be a sign unto you; Ye shall find the babe wrapped in swaddling clothes, lying in a manger."

Jesus was born in a humble stable among very ordinary people to powerfully demonstrate that salvation is accessible to any person who sincerely seeks him.

(Luke 2:11, 12)

"And I saw a great white throne, and him that sat on it, from whose face the earth and the heaven fled away; and there was found no place for them."

"And I saw the dead, small and great, stand before God; and the books were opened, which is the book of life: and the dead were judged out of those things which were written in the books, according to their works."

"And the sea gave up the dead which were in it; and death and hell delivered up the dead which were in them: and they were judged every man according to their works."

"And death and hell were cast into the lake of fire. This is the second death."

"And whosoever was not found written in the book of life was cast into the lake of fire."

"AND I saw a new heaven and a new earth: for the first heaven and the first earth were passed away; and there was no more sea."

"And I John saw the holy city, new Jerusalem, coming down from God out of heaven, prepared as a bride adorned for her husband."

"And I heard a great voice out of heaven saying, Behold, the tabernacle of God is with men, and he will dwell with them, and they shall be his people, and God himself shall be with them, and be their God."

And the dead were judged according to the things written in the books.

Salvation is accessible to all, but a time will come when it will be past the point where it is possible (too late) to receive it.

(Revelation 20:11-21:3)

99. How can I be sure of my salvation?

"Who are kept by the power of God through faith unto salvation ready to be revealed in the last time."

And God, in his mighty power, will protect you until you receive this salvation.

Salvation brings the sure hope of eternal life.

(I Peter 1:5)

"Therefore, brethren, we are debtors, not to the flesh, to live after the flesh."

"For if ye live after the flesh, ye shall die: but if ye through the Spirit do mortify the deeds of the body, ye shall live."

"For as many as are led by the Spirit of God, they are the sons of God."

"For ye have not received the spirit of bondage again to fear; but ye have received the Spirit of adoption, whereby we cry, Ab'-ba, Father."

"The Spirit itself beareth witness with our spirit, that we are the children of God:"

"And if the children, then heirs; heirs of God, and joint-heirs with Christ; if so be that we suffer with him, that we may be also glorified together."

All persons led by the Spirit of God are children of God.

The Holy Spirit takes residence in our hearts and assures us we are God's children.

(Romans 8:12-17)

"And when he had sent the multitudes away, he went up into a mountain apart to pray:

and when the evening was come, he was there alone."

"But the ship was now in the midst of the sea, tossed with waves; for the wind was contrary."

"And in the fourth watch of the night Jesus went unto them, walking on the sea."

"And when the disciples saw him walking on the sea, they were troubled, saying, It is a spirit; and they cried out for fear."

"But straightway Jesus spake unto them, saying, Be of good cheer; it is I; be not afraid."

"And Peter answered him and said, Lord, if it be thou, bid me come unto thee on the water."

"And he said, Come. And when Peter was come down out of the ship, he walked on the water, to go to Jesus."

"But when he saw the wind boisterous, he was afraid; and beginning to sink, he cried, saying, Lord, save me."

"And immediately Jesus stretched forth his hand, and caught him, and said unto him, O thou of little faith, wherefore didst thou doubt?"

"And when they were come into the ship, the wind ceased."

"Then they that were in the ship came and worshipped him, saying, Of a truth thou art the Son of God."

We cannot save ourselves from sin, guilt, judgment, and spiritual death. Only Jesus Christ can save us.

(Matthew 14:23-33)

100. Why is salvation so central to Christianity?

"And God saw that the wickedness of man was great in the earth, and that every imagination of the thoughts of his heart was only evil continually."

"And it repented the LORD that he had made man on the earth, and it grieved him at his heart."

"And the LORD said, I will destroy man whom I have created from the face of the earth; both man, and beast, and the creeping thing, and the fowls of the air; for it repenteth me that I have made them."

"But Noah found grace in the eyes of the LORD."

"These are the generations of Noah: Noah was a just man and perfect in his generations, and Noah walked with God."

"And Noah begat three sons, Shem, Ham, Ja'-pheth."

"The earth also was corrupt before God, and the earth was filled with violence."

"And God looked upon the earth, and, behold, it was corrupt; for all flesh had corrupted his way upon the earth."

"And God said unto Noah, The end of all flesh is come before me; for the earth is filled with violence through them; and, behold, I will destroy them with the earth."

"Make thee an ark of go'-pher wood; rooms shalt thou make in the ark, and shalt pitch it within and without with pitch."

"And this is the fashion which thou shalt make it of: The length of the ark shall be three cubits, the breadth of it fifty cubits, and the height of it thirty cubits."

"A window shalt thou make to the ark, and in a cubit shalt thou finish it above; and the door of the ark shalt thou set in the side thereof; with lower, second, and third stories shalt thou make it."

"And, behold, I, even I, do bring a flood of waters upon the earth, to destroy all flesh, wherein is the breath of life, from under heaven; and every thing that is in the earth shall die."

"But with thee will I establish my covenant; and thou shalt come into the ark, thou, and thy sons, and thy wife, and they sons' wives with thee."

"And of every living thing of all flesh, two of every sort shalt thou bring into the ark, to keep them alive with thee; they shall be male and female."

"Of fowls after their kind, and of cattle after their kind, of every creeping thing of the earth after his kind, two of every sort shall come unto thee, to keep them alive."

"And take thou unto thee of all food that is eaten, and thou shalt gather it to thee; and it shall be for food for thee, and for them."

"Thus did Noah, according to all that God commanded him, so did he."

(Genesis 6:5-22)

"For the wages of sin is death; but the gift of God is eternal life through Jesus Christ our Lord."

Salvation is necessary because sin against a holy God separates us from him, bringing judgment and spiritual death.

(Romans 6:23)

"AND the LORD spake unto Moses and Aaron in the land of Egypt, saying,"

"This month shall be unto you the beginning of months: it shall be the first month of the year to you."

"Speak ye unto all the congregation of Israel, saying, In the tenth day of this month they shall take to them every man a lamb, according to the house of their fathers, a lamb for an house:"

"And if the household be too little for the lamb, let him and his neighbour next unto his house take it according to the number of the souls; every man according to his eating shall make your count for the lamb."

"Your lamb shall be without blemish, a male of the first year: ye shall take it out from the sheep, or from the goats:"

"And ye shall keep it up until the fourteenth day of the same month: and the whole assembly of the congregation of Israel shall kill it in the evening."

"And they shall take of the blood, and strike it on the two side post and on the upper door post of the houses, wherein they shall eat it."

"And they shall eat the flesh in that night, roast with fire, and unleavened bread; and with bitter herbs they shall eat it."

"Eat not of it raw, nor sodden at all with water, but roast with fire; his head with his legs, and with the purtenance thereof."

"And ye shall let nothing of it remain until morning; and that which remaineth of it until the morning ye shall burn with fire."

"And thus shall ye eat it; with your lions girded, your shoes on your feet, and your staff in your hand; and ye shall eat it in haste: it is the LORD'S passover."

"For I will pass through the land of Egypt this night, and will smite all the firstborn in the land of Egypt, both man and beast; and against all the gods of Egypt I will execute judgment: I am the LORD."

"And the blood shall be to you for a token upon the houses where ye are: and when I see the blood, I will pass over you, and the plague shall not be upon you to destroy you, when I smite the land of Egypt."

"And this day shall be unto you for a memorial; and ye shall keep it a feast to the LORD throughout your generations; ye shall keep it a feast by an ordinance for ever."

"Seven days shall ye eat unleavened bread; even the first day ye shall put away leaven out of your houses: for whosoever eateth leavened bread from the first day until the seventh day, that soul shall be cutt off from Israel."

"And in the first day there shall be an holy convocation, and in the seventh day there shall be an holy convocation to you; no manner of work shall be done in them, save that which every man must eat, that only may be done of you."

"And ye shall observe the feast of unleavened bread; for in this self same day have I brought your armies out of the land of Egypt: therefore shall ye observe this day in your generations by an ordinance for ever."

"In the first month, on the fourteenth day of the month at even, ye shall eat unleavened bread, until the one and twentieth day of the month at even."

"Seven days shall there be no leaven found in your houses: for whosoever eateth that which is leavened, even that soul shall be cut off from the congregation of Israel, whether he be a stranger, or born in the land."

"Ye shall eat nothing leavened; in all your habitations shall ye eat unleavened bread."

"Then Moses called for all the elders of Israel, and said unto them, Draw out and take you a lamb according to your families, and kill the passover."

"And ye shall take a bunch of hyssop, and dip it in the blood that is in the bason, and strike the lintel and the two side posts with the blood that is in the bason; and none of you shall go out at the door of his house until the morning."

"For the LORD will pass through to smite the Egyptians; and when he seeth the blood upon the lintel, and on the two side posts, the LORD will pass over the door, and will not suffer the destroyer to come in unto your houses to smite you."

"And ye shall observe this thing for an ordinance to thee and to thy sons for ever."

"And it shall come to pass, when ye be come to the land which the LORD will give you, according as he hath promised, that ye shall keep this service."

"And it shall come to pass, when your children shall say unto you, What mean ye by this service?"

"That ye shall say, It is the sacrifice of the LORD's passover, who passed over the houses of the children of Israel in Egypt, when he smote the Egyptians, and delivered our houses. And the people bowed the head and worshipped."

Salvation through Christ is dramatically foreshadowed through the Passover lamb.

(Exodus 12:1-27)

"Neither is there salvation in any other: for there is none other name under heaven given among men, whereby we must be saved."

There is salvation in no one else! There is no other name in all of heaven for people to call on to save them.

In spite of the fact that it might sound exclusive, the Bible's claim of "ONE WAY" to salvation is really an expression of the grace and kindness of God.

(Acts 4:12)

PROMISE FROM GOD

"That if thou shalt confess with thy mouth the LORD Jesus, and shalt believe in thine heart that God hath raised him from the dead, thou shalt be saved."

(Romans 10:9)

Bibliography

THE HOLY BIBLE (1964) Authorized King James Version. Chicago, Ill.: J. G. Ferguson

The Holy Bible (1982) New International Version. Grand Rapids, MI.: Thomas Nelson (Used By Permission)

The Holy Bible (1978) New York, NY.: New York International Bible Society (Used By Permission)

The Holy Bible (1953) The Revised Standard Version. Nashville, TN.: Thomas Nelson & Sons (Used By Permission)

The Holy Bible (1901) The American Standard Version. Nashville, TN.: Thomas Nelson (Used By Permission)

The Holy Bible (1959) The Berkeley Version. Grand Rapids, MI.: Zondervan (Used By Permission)

The Holy Bible (1977) The New American Standard Bible. USA.: The Lockman Foundation (Used By Permission)

The Holy Bible (1996) The New Living Translation. Wheaton, Ill.: Tyndale House Publishers (Used By Permission)

The New Testament In The Language Of The People (1937, 1949) Chicago, Ill.:

Charles B. Williams, Bruce Humphries, Inc, The Moody Bible Institute (Used By Permission)

The New Testament In Modern English (1958) New York, NY.: J. B. Phillips, Macmillan (Used By Permission)

The Wycliff Bible Commentary (1962, 1968) Nashville, TN.: Chicago, Ill.:

The Southwestern Company, The Moody Bible Institute Of Chicago

About The Author

THE REVEREND DR. JOHN Thomas Wylie is one who has dedicated his life to the work of God's Service, the service of others; and being a powerful witness for the Gospel of Our Lord and Savior Jesus Christ. Dr. Wylie was called into the Gospel Ministry June 1979, whereby in that same year he entered The American Baptist College of the American Baptist Theological Seminary, Nashville, Tennessee.

As a young Seminarian, he read every book available to him that would help him better his understanding of God as well as God's plan of Salvation and the Christian Faith. He made a commitment as a promising student that he would inspire others as God inspires him. He understood early in his ministry that we live in times where people question not only who God is; but whether miracles are real, whether or not man can make a change, and who the enemy is or if the enemy truly exists.

Dr. Wylie carried out his commitment to God, which has been one of excellence which led to his earning his Bachelors of Arts in Bible/Theology/Pastoral

Studies. Faithful and obedient to the call of God, he continued to matriculate in his studies earning his Masters of Ministry from Emmanuel Bible College, Nashville, Tennessee & Emmanuel Bible College, Rossville, Georgia. Still, inspired to please the Lord and do that which is well – pleasing in the Lord's sight, Dr. Wylie recently on March 2006, completed his Masters of Education degree with a concentration in Instructional Technology earned at The American Intercontinental University, Holloman Estates, Illinois. Dr. Wylie also previous to this, earned his Education Specialist Degree from Jones International University, Centennial, Colorado and his Doctorate of Theology from The Holy Trinity College and Seminary, St. Petersburg, Florida.

Dr. Wylie has served in the capacity of pastor at two congregations in Middle Tennessee and Southern Tennessee, as well as served as an Evangelistic Preacher, Teacher, Chaplain, Christian Educator, and finally a published author, writer of many great inspirational Christian Publications such as his first publication:

"Only One God: Who Is He?" – published August 2002 via formally 1ˢᵗ books library (which is now AuthorHouse Book Publishers located in Bloomington, Indiana & Milton Keynes, United

Kingdom) which caught the attention of **The Atlanta Journal Constitution Newspaper.**

Dr. Wylie is happily married to Angel G. Wylie, a retired Dekalb Elementary School teacher who loves to work with the very young children and who always encourages her husband to move forward in the Name of Jesus Christ. They have Four children, 11 grand-children and one great-grandson all of whom they are very proud. Both Dr. Wylie and Angela Wylie serve as members of the Salem Baptist Church, located in Lilburn, Georgia, where the Reverend Dr. Richard B. Haynes is Senior pastor.

Dr. Wylie has stated of his wife: "she knows the charm and beauty of sincerity, goodness, and purity through Jesus Christ. Yes, she is a Christian and realizes the true meaning of loveliness as the reflection as her life of holy living gives new meaning, hope, and purpose to that of her husband, her children, others may say of her, "Behold the handmaiden of the Lord." A Servant of Jesus Christ!

Printed in the United States
By Bookmasters